FRUGAL FOOD

Delia Smith is one of the most po[pular co]okery experts writing today.

Justly famous for her phenomenally successful BBC TV series, *Delia Smith's Cookery Course*, she has a huge and devoted following.

On top of her television and newspaper journalism, she has delighted millions of cooks the world over with her many publications, including the classic paperbacks,
HOW TO CHEAT AT COOKING,
THE EVENING STANDARD COOKBOOK and
DELIA SMITH'S BOOK OF CAKES—all available from Coronet.

Frugal Food

Delia Smith

Illustrations by Vanessa Pancheri

CORONET BOOKS
Hodder and Stoughton

*First published in Great Britain 1976 by
Coronet Books Limited*

Twelfth impression 1984

Printed and bound in Great Britain for
Hodder and Stoughton Paperbacks, a
division of Hodder and Stoughton Ltd.,
Mill Road, Dunton Green, Sevenoaks, Kent
(Editorial Office: 47 Bedford Square,
London, WC1 3DP) by
Richard Clay (The Chaucer Press) Ltd.,
Bungay, Suffolk

ISBN 0 340 21002 8

All author's royalties from the sale of this book will go to Christian Aid and the Catholic Fund for Overseas Development.

My thanks to Colin Fisher of the Pye Research Centre, Haughley, Suffolk, for his invaluable, comments: to Gwyneth Phillips for typing the manuscript: and, as always, to Caroline Liddell for her help with the testing.

CONTENTS

PREFACE

You may be wondering how it is that a cookery writer who spends a great deal of her time encouraging people to eat perhaps a little more adventurously than they normally would could at the same time have any leanings towards frugality. The fact is I feel our days of unrestricted choice in eating are strictly numbered. There simply isn't enough food on this planet to feed all the people who live on it: rich nations like our own are just beginning to feel the pinch, while two-thirds of the world's population continues to suffer from the grave effects of living below subsistence level.

It is a paradox which concerns me personally a great deal. Ultimately perhaps the problems will have to be solved on an international level, but governments only reflect the will of the people they govern. As individuals, are there really any of us who, if we found ourselves living next door to a family whose children were starving, would not give all the help we could? But the truth is we *are* living next door, on the next continent, on the same planet.

This book has been prompted partly by these considerations and partly by the practical point that in the future there will be less food around (at least of the kind we have been accustomed to)—something that is not entirely unwelcome. One doesn't have to be a nutritionist to realise that our eating habits have got somewhat out of hand, with obesity and the diseases attributable to it having reached epidemic proportions. I feel the positive effect of this in time will be a material improvement in our health, as in the war years when we ate so much less. Also, believe it or not, I do feel that the less you have of something, the more special it is—so you enjoy it more. We shall still be well-off compared with the greater part of the world, which is not to say that we should feel guilty about cooking good food but rather that we should have some sort of responsibility to make the most of it and not squander it.

INTRODUCTION

Anyone who wants to, or is forced to, live *really* frugally (that is to say, at subsistence level) has no need of a cookbook. And at the same time I'm quite sure there are many people who, because they are careful, can live more frugally than this book would suggest.

Who, then, is this book for? Quite simply for people like myself, those who have lived and cooked through the last twenty affluent years and now find themselves caught up in the spiral of inflation, rising prices and impending world food shortages.

In short, it's a *start*. If you wish to trim your cooking (and spending) wings a bit, start here. It's quite easy, quite fun and, if my experience in preparing and writing this book is anything to go by, it's really not half so morbid an exercise as you might think. In fact, once you become really calculating, boring old shopping can take on a new meaning.

No more will you simply go through the motions of loading up the supermarket trolley and day-dreaming in dreary check-out queues. You'll go forth into battle fortified, as it were, by the armour of your new-found attention to frugality! The seductive cunning of commercials will now meet its match—in you. Nothing will be tossed lightly into your basket: you'll know how much it weighs, what it costs, *and* how much it cost last week.

You haven't got the time? I know, I said it too. But suddenly I didn't have the money to save all this time we've become so besotted with. Actually I'm not so sure that all this time-saving really does save time. I once watched a lady standing in a long check-out queue with just a large bag of frozen brussels sprouts (they were at the time about 30 per cent dearer than the fresh ones). She was in the queue for a good 10 or 12 minutes; she could, had she so wished, have sat in her own kitchen and peeled fresh brussels sprouts in the same time. Then take something like tea bags: they'll save you the bother of emptying tea leaves—whatever small amount of time that involves—but you'll pay twice the price for your tea.

However, before we start cooking, here are a few tips on thinking frugally.

THE CHEAP CHARTER

1 *Your money or your time* Really this is what is at the root of many of our economic predicaments. 'Labour-saving' was the slogan of the 'sixties: leave it all to the kitchen gadgets, the machines, the tins and packets, and put your feet up. Well, even if you overlook the psychological repercussions for bored (if liberated) housewives, consider the economic implications for a minute. First of all, instant foods cost a fortune. Secondly, all those super gadgets cost a fortune—and then they break down, and when they do it's ten to one you can't get the mending-man to come. 'Are you north or south Suffolk, madam?' 'Oh, you're in the middle. He won't be in your area for ten days.' So off you go to the launderette, get a £6 parking ticket, plus £8 for the repair man when he comes ten days later and £6 for the spare part. Just one (real-life) example of how much saved labour we have to pay for. The same applies to cooking: if you are willing to spend the *time*, you are bound to save money.

2 *Getting out of the supermarket and back into the kitchen*   So our bored, liberated housewife needs a job (*a*) to pay for her labour-saving home and (*b*) to pay the interest. With the result that on Friday nights and Saturdays the supermarkets are packed with rushed, harassed, working wives and mothers stocking up on instant puds, apple pies, sponge cakes, frozen hamburgers, fish fingers and packaged meat, to name but a few expensive items. A few years ago I wrote a book to enable people to make the very best of all these things. But in the meantime our priorities, I feel, have been changing, and it is the kitchen now that demands more of our time and imagination. Hence the aim of this book—to make that time spent as interesting and worthwhile as possible.

3 *Seasonal sense*   I need hardly mention how the price of oil has affected everything we consume, but just *think* how much more it now costs to fly all those tasteless out-of-season fruits and vegetables merely so we can choose whatever we want every single week of the year! Not only has all this jet-set food eclipsed the natural cycles of our diet, but also it has become so much harder to decide what to cook when there's absolutely everything to choose from. Nature is perfectly capable of providing us with a varied and interesting diet throughout the year, and by buying things in their natural season you'll be getting them at their most plentiful and therefore at their cheapest. In June a few ungraded asparagus spears can be far cheaper than imported celery; in December home-grown celery is much less expensive (and has far more flavour) than a pound of imported tomatoes. And, personally, I enjoy the fun of anticipation—I long for the first tender young peas, and

equally I look forward to the (so underrated) root vegetables of winter.

4 *Anti freeze* Well, I'm afraid I am, although I admit it's a personal thing largely for the reasons outlined above. Also I'm not convinced freezing does always save money. Each time I am reminded that 20 per cent of the population are freezer-owners I console myself with the thought that there are still 80 per cent who are not. My main grumble is that unless you understand temperature control with almost scientific dedication freezing causes *loss of flavour*, and as a cook I spend a great deal of time and effort nurturing flavour. One report in a consumer magazine pointed out that very often freezer families spent more on meat than other families—they bought more than they normally would in order to justify the freezer, and of course when buying whole sides they were landed with far more heads, tails and ears than they needed. Having said all this, it is true you *can* save a little money with fruit and vegetables, if you grow these yourself and produce too much for your immediate needs. If you already have a freezer and it's saving you money, it can't be a bad thing. On the other hand, if you don't have one and are thinking about it, do ask yourself if you really want to eat your courgettes and strawberries in January and your red cabbage in June.

5 *Saving it* Energy has become a fashionable word of late. Before that saving kitchen energy meant sitting down to shell the peas. When the Government first urged us daily to switch something off, we listened a bit; then the enormous increases in charges started arriving through our letter-boxes and we listened a lot. After water and heating, the oven is the highest consumer of energy in the house, and heating up the whole capacity of the oven just to cook a quiche is no longer feasible. No doubt you all have devised ways of saving energy in the kitchen, but here anyway are a few suggestions.

(*a*) Keep the kettle regularly de-scaled—it will boil quicker.

(*b*) Invest in a steamer and cook one vegetable on top of another on the same heat.

(*c*) When baking jacket potatoes, push a skewer through the centres as this conducts the heat to the insides and speeds up the cooking time.

(*d*) Invest in an electric toaster—it uses far less energy than the grill.

(*e*) Try to use the oven to its capacity by planning to use it for more than one thing (e.g. baking in a batch, cooking two casseroles or cooking vegetables and soups in the oven if it's on).

(*f*) If you are buying a new oven, consider a double one so that you can use the smaller oven for most things and probably cut costs by half.

6 *A touch of spice* One way to prevent life getting dull when you're saving money on cooking is to stock up with a few herbs and spices. Don't get me wrong: throwing in a hotch-potch of this and that is definitely not recommended. It is the subtle addition that adds a touch of luxury to the simplest dishes. First and foremost (I'll say it yet again), do invest in a pepper-mill. Freshly ground black pepper adds a new dimension instantly to your cooking. Also keep some untreated pure rock salt (such as Maldon) in your spice cupboard—it's more expensive than table salt but, because it's saltier, it goes further. Coarsely ground black pepper and a sprinkling of crushed rock salt can put something like egg and chips in the four-star class! Spices are cheaper sold loose or in packets (from Boots). Why pay for fancy jars? At the same time pester your local delicatessen or wholefood shop for unusual spices—the more we ask, the more we're likely to get them (if you do have trouble locating any spices, Robert Jackson Piccadilly, London W1, will send them out by post if you write for the prices etc.).

Green-fingered cooks, or even those who aren't (like me), should be able to grow fresh herbs, either in the garden or on a sunny windowsill in pots. Clare Lowenfield's book *Herb Gardening* is very informative.

Finally, one thing that I get a lot of letters about is olive oil and its price. At the time of writing it's about £7 a gallon, which is cheaper than buying it by the pint but still very expensive. Undoubtedly the best alternative is groundnut oil (Sainsburys sell a good one), and I like it because it has little flavour of its own and therefore doesn't mask other flavours, like some abominable oils on the market at present. Groundnut oil is good for frying—and add a knob of butter for flavour.

I also use groundnut oil in salad dressing and in mayonnaise with a little crushed garlic added, again for flavour. If you have some precious olive oil, you can make it go further by adding 50 per cent groundnut oil to it. For my vinaigrette dressing I use 1 tablespoon of wine or cider vinegar, 6–7 tablespoons of oil, 1 crushed clove of garlic, 1 teaspoon of mustard, 1 teaspoon of crushed rock salt and freshly milled black pepper—then I shake everything together vigorously in a screw-top jar. In the summer a few chopped herbs will give it an extra-special flavour.

7 How to cook without wine I think it was Elizabeth David, one of our greatest cookery writers, who once said that if the British spent as much money on wine in the kitchen as they do on gravy powder, meat cubes and instant stock they would all enjoy better food. Well, I heartily endorse that, but just as all those chemically flavoured aids have gone up in price, so too has wine. But, again prompted by Mrs. David, I have discovered that a very good alternative to wine in the kitchen is dry cider. In fact, I now rarely use wine, but I always have some dry cider handy for special dishes. I've experimented quite a lot and have found that a classic coq au vin or even boeuf bourguignonne (see the version on p. 87) has turned out beautifully with cider. If you can, try to get hold of some Aspall Hall still dry cider—this is the best of all for cooking.

8 A question of cream As a cookery writer I can say quite confidently that nothing seems to get people's economical backs up quite as much as cream in cooking. It's perfectly all right to spend money on smoking, or crisps, or bars of choco- late, but cooking with cream is considered by some to be the ultimate in kitchen extravagance. One lady was outraged, I recall, by my making a bread and butter pudding on television with cream; I ought to have been teaching people to economise in this day and age. Well, perhaps in the context of this book the appearance of a little cream here and there does call for an explanation. For me, quite simply, cream is the one ingredient that makes frugality tolerable! If you like, you can substitute top of the milk for it.

9 *What are we leaving?*   In one American university there is, would you believe, a department of Garbageology which regularly 'borrows' people's dustbins and analyses their contents. They claim that it tells us a great deal about our modern way of life. In one American city they discovered that the average family wasted 10–15 per cent of all the food it bought (amounting in the whole city, over the year, to $10 million worth of food thrown away). And that was not bones, scraps or peelings but large pieces of once perfectly edible bread and meat, as well as unopened packs of vegetables and television dinners. They even found that, as the price of meat soared, so did the wastage! I mention all this only to underline the obvious point that frugality calls for good management, and an enthusiastic approach to leftovers (for which you'll find some recipes later). It would be a tragic waste of that extra time we're going to spend in the kitchen if 15 per cent of the food was thrown away afterwards.

Luxury SOUPS

So how can we be at once frugal and luxurious, you're thinking? Easy. Luxuries are rarities—foie gras and caviare cost a fortune because they're scarce. When oysters were ten-a-penny (as indeed they were in the last century) they were merely food of the poor: now they're right up in the luxury class.

One of the rarest things in these days of instant living, in my opinion, is real homemade soup made with real homemade stock—and for me that makes it a luxury. At least this state of affairs has a positive side for us frugal cooks, because now we can offer our family or friends luxury at a very small cost.

I'll go even further. If you've got an attractive tureen full of comforting, inviting homemade soup on the table—with homemade bread, butter, a hunk of cheese and some fruit—who's going to notice the absence of meat or fish or any other main course? In this chapter I've chosen, for the most part, substantial and filling soups, and just a couple of lighter ones with the summer months in mind.

Basic Stock

4 lb beef shin bones (in pieces)
1 lb veal knuckle bones (in pieces)
1 Spanish onion peeled and quartered
2 celery stalks (plus leaves) cut into halves
2 large carrots peeled and cut into large chunks
1 bayleaf
1 small bunch parsley stalks
10 whole black peppercorns
1 blade of mace
1 heaped teaspoon salt
1 level teaspoon sugar

Pre-heat the oven to mark 8/450°F

First of all place the bones in a meat roasting tin together with the onion and carrot, and place the tin on the highest shelf in the oven and leave it for about 45 minutes to allow the bones and vegetables to brown—turning them now and then so that they brown evenly. Then have some boiling water ready, and transfer the bones, the onion and carrots to a cooking-pot (about 6 quarts capacity).

Add seven pints of water to the pot, along with the celery, bay leaf, mace, peppercorns and parsley stalks, and bring the liquid very slowly up to simmering point before adding the salt and sugar. Skim off any scum that has come to the surface, partly cover and simmer as gently as possible for 4 to 5 hours (partly covering the pot by putting the lid half on will ensure the liquid reduces to give the stock a more concentrated flavour).

When it's ready, strain into a clean pan and leave to cool. When the stock is quite cold you can then remove the layer of fat that will have formed on the top (and keep this for dripping). The stock is now ready for use: the bones can either be discarded or topped up with more water. This is a basic brown beef stock—for a light stock, use all veal bones instead of beef and dispense with the browning in the oven.

Goulash Soup with Dumplings   (Serves 4–6)

1 lb shin of beef
2 tablespoons beef dripping
1 large onion, peeled and chopped
2 tablespoons flour
1 tablespoon Hungarian paprika
¼ teaspoon dried marjoram
½ teaspoon caraway seeds
1 clove garlic, crushed
A 14-oz tin tomatoes
1 teaspoon tomato purée
1½ pints beef stock
1 lb potatoes, peeled and cut into cubes
1 green pepper, de-seeded and chopped
¼ pint soured cream or yoghurt
Salt and freshly milled black pepper

For the dumplings:
4 oz self-raising flour
2 oz shredded suet
Salt and freshly milled black pepper

Trim and cut the meat into very small pieces, then heat the beef dripping in a large pan and fry the meat over a high heat until well browned. Now lower the heat a little, stir in the onion and cook until it's lightly browned. Sprinkle in the flour, paprika, marjoram, caraway seeds and garlic. Stir well and cook for a minute or two before adding the tomatoes and stock. When it comes to simmering point, cover and continue simmering very gently for 45 minutes. After that, take the lid off and stir in the tomato purée, followed by the potatoes and chopped pepper, and simmer gently for 10 minutes, stirring occasionally. Then in a bowl, mix the flour and shredded suet, season with salt and pepper, and add enough cold water to make a smooth elastic dough. Divide the dough into 12 small dumplings, pop them on to the soup—don't press them down, though, just let them float. Then put the lid back on and simmer for a further 25 minutes. Taste to check the seasoning and add a dollop of soured cream or yoghurt to each serving.

Split Pea and Vegetable Soup   (Serves 6)

Yellow or green split peas will do for this deliciously thick and substantial soup.

½ lb green split peas
4 oz streaky bacon, rinded and chopped small
1 medium onion, peeled and chopped
2 sticks celery, chopped
1 large carrot, scraped and chopped
½ small turnip, peeled and chopped
½ small swede, peeled and chopped
3 oz butter or bacon fat
3 pints stock (or water)
Salt and freshly milled black pepper

First, in a large cooking pot, melt the fat, then cook the bacon and onion in it for 5 minutes before adding the rest of the vegetables—give them a good stir round in the butter and let them colour a little at the edges over a fairly low heat. Then pour in the stock and add the washed split peas. Bring everything back to simmering point, skim the surface if there's any scum, then put a lid on and continue to simmer very gently for about 1½ hours, or until the peas are absolutely soft. Now liquidise the soup just a little (or else sieve it)—but it shouldn't be too uniformly smooth. Taste, season, re-heat and serve the soup garnished with some croutons crisp-fried in bacon fat.

Note: There's no need to soak the split peas, but the length of cooking time may vary 30 minutes or so either way.

Thick Country Soup

(Serves 6–8)

I say thick, because you could stand your spoon up in this one!
If you prefer it a little thinner, just add more liquid, to your
taste.

½ lb dried haricot beans
2 tablespoons oil
1 onion, peeled and chopped
2 cloves garlic, crushed
2 sticks celery, chopped
2 carrots, scraped and chopped
4 oz streaky bacon, rinded and chopped
2 leeks, cleaned thoroughly, trimmed, halved lengthways and
    sliced into ¼-inch thick rings
3 courgettes, unpeeled but trimmed each end and chopped
½ small head Savoy cabbage, shredded
2 teaspoons dried basil
4 oz raw, long-grain rice
4 tablespoons tomato purée
Salt and freshly milled black pepper

First, put the beans into a saucepan with 3 pints of cold water,
bring to the boil and boil for 2–3 minutes. Then turn the heat
off, put a lid on and leave on one side for about an hour, to
soak. Towards the end of that time, heat the oil in a large pan
and gently fry the onions, garlic, celery, carrots and bacon
together for about 10–15 minutes. Now return to the soaked
beans and bring them back to the boil with the lid on and
simmer for about 30 minutes, or until the beans are tender.
Then, using a draining spoon, scoop out about half the beans
and transfer them to an electric blender. Measure and add a
pint of their cooking water and blend until smooth; then pour
this on to the softened vegetables and add the remaining whole
beans and their cooking water together with the prepared leeks,
courgettes, cabbage, basil and a further pint of water. Bring it
all to the boil, add the tomato purée and sprinkle in the rice.
Stir well, then cover and simmer very gently for 30 minutes.
Finally, taste and season well with salt and freshly milled
pepper.

German Soup with Frankfurters (Serves 4-6)

This soup is made more substantial by the addition of bacon and frankfurters.

2 pints stock—preferably homemade
2 medium potatoes, peeled and diced
4 leeks
½ lb turnips
½ lb carrots
1 stick celery
4 oz streaky bacon, rinded and chopped
4 long frankfurters (or 6 small)
Salt and freshly milled black pepper

Pour the stock into a largish saucepan with the diced potatoes and bring to the boil; then cover and simmer gently until the potatoes are soft—that should be in about 10 minutes. While that is happening, start to prepare the vegetables: first the leeks, which should be slit open lengthways and then cut across in ¼-inch slices. Wash them in several changes of water to get rid of the dust, then drain in a colander. Now take a sharp knife and peel and dice the root vegetables into quite small pieces, and cut up the celery too. The chopped bacon should be fried without any additional fat until it's fairly crisp. Then, as soon as the potato is soft, rub it through a sieve (or liquidise it) and return it to the saucepan together with the vegetables, bacon and any fat that came out of it. Now bring the soup up to a gentle simmer, taste and add some seasoning, then cover and cook gently for about an hour. The frankfurters should be sliced thinly and stirred into the soup to heat through gently just a few minutes before you serve it. Then serve it very hot.

Soupe Les Halles

(Serves 6)

2 tablespoons butter
2 tablespoons oil
1½ lb onions, peeled and thinly sliced
2 cloves garlic, crushed
½ teaspoon granulated sugar
2½ pints good beef stock
6 slices French bread (baked till crisp for about 20 minutes
   in a medium oven)
Extra butter
8 oz grated Cheddar or Lancashire cheese
Salt and freshly milled black pepper

Heat the butter and oil together in a large saucepan. Stir in the
sliced onions, garlic and sugar, and cook over a fairly low heat
for about 30 minutes, or until the base of the pan is covered
with a nutty brown, caramelised film (this browning process is
important as it improves the colour of the resulting soup and
also helps considerably with the flavour). Now pour on the
stock, bring the soup to the boil, cover and simmer gently for
about an hour. Then taste the soup and season with salt and
freshly milled black pepper, and pre-heat the grill. Now spread
the slices of baked French bread with butter. Place each slice
in a fireproof soup bowl, ladle the soup on top, and when the
bread surfaces sprinkle grated cheese over the top of each bowl.
Now place the bowls under a hot grill until the cheese is
browned and bubbling.

Potage Flamande

This is nicest made with young brussels sprouts in November
—hopefully after a good frost.

¾ lb potatoes
2 leeks
¾ lb brussels sprouts
2 oz butter
½ pint stock
1 pint milk
2 tablespoons top of the milk
Salt and freshly milled black pepper
A squeeze of lemon juice
4 rashers streaky bacon, rinded and grilled

Peel and slice the potatoes first; then halve the leeks lengthways, slice them across fairly thickly and wash and drain them
thoroughly. Then trim the bases of the sprouts and discard
any damaged outer leaves. Now quarter the larger sprouts and
halve the smaller ones. Next melt the butter in a good large
saucepan. Add the potatoes, leeks and sprouts, and stir well to
coat them nicely in the butter. Cover and cook gently for 5
minutes, then add the stock and milk. Bring to simmering
point, cover and cook *very* gently for 20–25 minutes, or until
the potatoes are soft. Now liquidise or sieve the soup and
return it to the pan; add the top of the milk, then re-heat the
soup gently, taste and season with salt and freshly milled
pepper, and add a squeeze of lemon juice. The bacon should be
grilled until absolutely crisp, then crumbled into the soup
before serving.

Note: Instead of the top of the milk and lemon juice, you
could add ¼ pint of soured cream—depending on your budget
at the time!

Potage Paysanne

I often make this with the stock left over from boiling a bacon joint.

1–2 pints stock (or 1 of stock and 1 of water)
¼ medium turnip, peeled
½ small swede, peeled
2 carrots, scraped
2 sticks celery
2 medium onions, peeled
1 large or 2 small leeks, trimmed and washed
A good handful of green brussels tops (or the inner leaves
   of a green cabbage)
2 teaspoons tomato purée
1 clove garlic, crushed
2–3 oz dripping (preferably bacon fat)
Salt and freshly milled black pepper

First take a chopping board and a sharp knife and peel and chop all the vegetables very finely—the soup is not going to be sieved, so it's important that the vegetables are cut very small. Now take a large cooking pot, melt the fat and stir in all the chopped vegetables except the brussels tops. Stir them round and round to get a good coating of fat, then add the garlic, put a lid on and let them sweat over a low heat for about 15 minutes—don't worry if they turn a little golden round the edges, but *do* stir them now and then to prevent them sticking. After that, pour in the stock and add the tomato purée. Cover again and simmer gently for 45 minutes, then add the shredded greens. Taste and season with salt and freshly milled pepper, and cook for a further 10 minutes, this time without a lid.

Cream of Celery Soup   (Serves 4-6)

I think this is a delicious soup—best made with English celery after a good November frost.

¾ lb sticks celery, trimmed (save the leaves)
¼ lb potatoes, peeled and cut into chunks
2 medium leeks (white parts only), sliced and washed
1 pint chicken stock
½ pint milk
2 tablespoons cream
¼ teaspoon celery seeds
Salt and freshly milled black pepper
1 oz butter

Melt the butter in a large pan over a low heat. Chop the celery and add it to the pan, together with the potatoes and drained leeks. Then stir to coat the vegetables with butter, cover and cook very gently for about 15 minutes, shaking the pan from time to time to prevent the vegetables from sticking. Next pour in the stock and milk, and sprinkle in the celery seeds and some salt. Bring to simmering point, then cover and cook over a very low heat (watching it doesn't boil over) for 20–25 minutes, or until the vegetables are absolutely tender. Then liquidise or sieve the soup, return the purée to the pan and add the cream. Bring back to the boil, taste, add salt and freshly milled pepper, then just before serving chop up any reserved celery leaves and stir them into the soup.

Carrot and Leek Soup   (Serves 4 as a main course)

This makes a nice change from the more usual Leek and Potato Soup, provided of course the carrots are not too expensive.

1 lb leeks
1 lb carrots
1 medium onion
1 clove garlic, crushed
1 oz dripping
2½ pints stock
A dash of Worcestershire sauce
Salt and freshly milled black pepper

First of all prepare the vegetables. The leeks should be trimmed, leaving as much green as possible, then halved lengthways, chopped and washed in plenty of cold water. Then scoop them into a colander to drain. Next peel the carrots and cut them into smallish pieces—and the same goes for the onion. Now take a large saucepan, heat the dripping and add all the prepared vegetables along with the crushed clove of garlic. Stir them around a bit, then cover and 'sweat' them for 10 minutes over a low heat, shaking the pan from time to time. Next pour in the stock, add some seasoning, bring to simmering point, cover and simmer very gently for about 10 minutes, or until the pieces of carrot are tender. Now either sieve or liquidise the soup, then return it to the pan, taste to check the seasoning, add a few drops of Worcester sauce and re-heat gently. If you happen to have some Parmesan cheese handy, a little would be very nice sprinkled on each serving.

Potato Soup with Bacon   (Serves 4)

This is a thick, very warming soup, just right when the weather is cold.

1 lb potatoes, peeled and chopped
2 large carrots, scraped and chopped
2 sticks celery, chopped
1 small turnip, peeled and chopped
1 medium onion, peeled and chopped
2 oz butter or dripping
2 pints stock
½ teaspoon dried marjoram
2 rashers streaky bacon, rinded
Salt and freshly milled black pepper

Take a large thick-based saucepan and melt the butter or dripping over a very gentle heat. Then add all the prepared vegetables, stirring them around to get them well coated with the fat. Cover with a well-fitting lid, and with the heat kept very low let the vegetables 'sweat' gently for about 15 minutes —if you give the pan a shake from time to time you won't have any trouble with the vegetables sticking. After 15 minutes pour in the stock and add the marjoram and some salt and pepper. Then put the lid almost back on but leave a ½-inch gap at the edge (to let some of the steam escape). Simmer the soup like this for about another 20 minutes, or until the vegetables are soft.

Now you can either sieve or liquidise half the contents of the saucepan, and then return them to the other half. This means that the soup will be thickened nicely and will still have some bits of vegetable in it for texture. Next, grill or fry the bacon rashers until crisp, and crumble them into the soup in little bits. I think this soup is nice served with some croutons crisp-fried in bacon fat.

Cauliflower Soup

(Serves 4 as a main course

As cauliflowers are available all the year round and prices tend
to fluctuate enormously, this soup is only really economical
when the price is right.

1 largish cauliflower
1 pint stock (a light chicken stock or just plain water)
1 pint milk
1 bayleaf
¾ lb potatoes, peeled and chopped small
A squeeze of lemon juice
Freshly grated nutmeg
Salt and freshly milled black pepper
1 tablespoon cream, top of the milk or soured cream
  (whatever's available)

First separate the florets of the cauliflower from the hard stalk
(this can be kept and grated for a salad). Now you need to
separate the florets themselves into very tiny pieces. Then in a
medium saucepan bring the stock and bayleaf to simmering
point, throw in the little pieces of cauliflower and simmer them
for about 6 minutes, or until they are just cooked but still have
some 'bite'. Lift them out with a draining spoon and keep them
on one side. Pour in the milk now and add the potatoes, then
simmer gently without a lid until the potatoes are soft—about
10 minutes. Next rub the soup through a sieve, or liquidise it,
and return it to the saucepan. Now return the cauliflower to the
saucepan and re-heat gently, adding a squeeze of lemon juice.
some salt and pepper, and a scraping of nutmeg. Then stir in
the cream just before serving.

Soupe aux Choux

(Serves 4–6)

The reason this has a French title is because, as well as being French inspired, 'Soupe aux Choux' sounds more promising than 'Bacon and Cabbage Soup'.

½ white cabbage
1 oz dripping or bacon fat
½ lb unsmoked streaky bacon, rinded and diced
2 medium onions, peeled and chopped
1 medium potato, peeled and chopped
1 leek, sliced and washed
1 clove garlic, crushed
3 pints stock
Salt and freshly milled black pepper
Freshly grated nutmeg

Prepare the cabbage by first cutting out any hard stalky bits or ribs and then shredding it as thinly as possible. Now blanch the cabbage by placing it in a saucepan of cold water, bringing it to the boil and boiling for 1 minute, after which it needs to be drained in a colander. Now, using the same saucepan, heat the fat and fry the bacon until the fat starts to run from it. Then add the onion, potato, leek and garlic, stir all the vegetables around, and cook them until softened and slightly golden. Next stir in the drained cabbage and cook for another minute or two before pouring in the stock. Bring it back to the boil and then simmer it very gently without a lid for about an hour. Finally taste and season with salt and pepper and a little freshly grated nutmeg.

EGGS AND US

Well actually the egg and I are great companions. I love them
pure and simple, as the advert says—in fact, I'm almost
obsessed with them, for ever stopping the car on country roads
and peeping over fences where the sign says 'Eggs For Sale'
just to see if the hens are running about, as my grandmother
puts it.

Alas, free-range is unrealistic nowadays, so mostly I make
do with the supermarket variety. Mind you, I'm just as
obsessive there too—because *fresh* certainly isn't unrealistic
and I'll always be grateful to the EEC for introducing packing

date-stamps on egg boxes. I no longer have to gaze and wonder how long they've been hanging about: it tells you. I suppose, if you're in a hurry, it *can* take a while to tot up which Week 34 is—but persevere, because if we have to eat battery eggs, then at least they must be fresh.

Once you have a few fresh eggs in the house you'll never be short of a quick cheap meal: there's something very reassuring about lightly boiled eggs served with 'soldiers' of brown bread and butter, and freshly made tea. However, in this chapter we're after something different—still the same good old standby eggs but made into main meals that won't cost much extra (but *taste* as if they did!).

Curried Egg Patties

(Serves 2)

This is good for an unexpected meal, provided you have half a dozen eggs in the house.

4 hardboiled eggs, chopped small
1 teaspoon tomato purée
½ teaspoon Worcestershire sauce
½ teaspoon lemon juice
2 oz butter
1½ oz flour
¼ pint milk
1 teaspoon Madras curry powder
1 teaspoon salt
1 egg, beaten
1 extra egg, beaten
Seasoned flour
Dried breadcrumbs
Oil for frying

Melt the butter in a saucepan, then stir in the flour, curry powder and salt. Cook for 2 minutes, then gradually stir in the milk to make a very thick sauce. Cook this for 5 minutes, stirring all the time, and then take the pan off the heat and add 1 beaten egg, the tomato purée, Worcestershire sauce and lemon juice. Now add the hardboiled eggs, stir to mix them in, then season with salt. Next transfer the mixture to a bowl, cover and chill until the mixture becomes firm. Then before cooking form the mixture into 4 little round cakes, about ¾ inch thick, and dip them first in the seasoned flour, then in the extra beaten egg and finally in the breadcrumbs. Now shallow fry them in ¼ inch of hot oil till golden brown and drain on kitchen paper before serving.

Poached Eggs with Soufflé'd Welsh Rarebit

4 fresh eggs for poaching
½ oz butter
½ oz flour
6 tablespoons milk
½ teaspoon French mustard
A dash of Worcestershire sauce
A little cayenne pepper
2 extra eggs, separated
1 oz strong Cheddar cheese, grated
1 oz grated Parmesan
6–8 slices white bread (medium thick)
Salt and freshly milled black pepper

First heat some water in a frying pan with a little salt ready to poach the eggs in. Then take a small saucepan, melt the butter in it, stir in the flour and cook over a medium heat for a minute or two before gradually stirring in the milk. Allow the mixture to bubble for 2 minutes, then take the saucepan off the heat and stir in the seasonings. Now separate the two extra eggs and beat the yolks; then stir the yolks into the sauce and leave the mixture until it's cold. Next beat in the grated cheeses. Whisk the egg whites until stiff and carefully fold them into the cheese mixture. Now toast the bread on both sides and cover each slice thickly with the cheese mixture. Cook under a medium grill until the cheese mixture is puffed up and dark brown on top. During the last part—whilst you grill the cheese mixture—slip the 4 eggs into simmering water to poach for 3 minutes. Lift them out with a draining spoon, resting it on kitchen paper to drain each egg, then pop one on each of the toasts.

Eggs with Cheese and Spinach Sauce

(Serves 2)

This is very colourful to look at and quite filling served with rice and a green salad.

½ lb fresh spinach leaves, cooked and drained, or ¼ lb frozen
    spinach (thawed)
4 large eggs
1 small onion, peeled and finely chopped
2 oz butter
1 oz flour
½ pint milk
3 oz grated Cheddar cheese
2 tablespoons cream
Salt and freshly milled pepper
Freshly grated nutmeg ·

Melt 1½ oz butter in a small saucepan and gently soften the onion in it for 10 minutes. Then stir in the flour, cook for a minute or two and add the milk a little at a time, stirring after each addition, to make a smooth sauce. Taste and season the sauce, and let it cook for 6 minutes over a very gentle heat. Meanwhile boil the eggs by placing them in cold water, bringing them up to the boil and simmering them for 6 minutes, afterwards cooling them under cold running water. Now add two-thirds of the grated cheese to the sauce, stir it in and allow it to melt; then transfer the sauce to a liquidiser, add the extra ½ oz butter, the cream and the chopped drained spinach, and whizz the sauce until it's a pale green colour and only very tiny speckles of the spinach are visible. Season the sauce again, adding some nutmeg. Peel the eggs now, then halve them. Put a layer of sauce in a buttered gratin dish and arrange the eggs on top, rounded side up. Cover with the rest of the sauce, sprinkle with the remainder of the grated cheese and place the dish under a hot grill until the cheese is brown and the sauce is bubbling.

Egg and Bacon Pie

(Serves 4)

I've always found the conventional egg and bacon pie a bit on the dry side: however, try it this way, you'll find it's a whole lot nicer.

For the shortcrust pastry:
6 oz plain flour
3 oz lard
A pinch each salt and pepper
Cold water to mix

For the filling:
4 large eggs
6 rashers lean streaky bacon, rinded
¼ pint milk
Salt and freshly milled black pepper

Pre-heat the oven to mark 6/400 °F with a baking sheet in it

First hardboil 3 of the eggs by placing them in a saucepan, covering them with cold water, bringing it up to the boil and simmering gently for 7 minutes; then cool them rapidly under cold running water. Next either grill or fry the bacon rashers gently until the fat starts to run. While they're cooking, and the eggs are cooling, make the pastry. Divide it in half, and use half to line a flan tin (if possible one with a rim). Now peel and chop the hardboiled eggs quite small, and chop the bacon fairly small as well. Next arrange the chopped bacon and eggs in the flan and season with freshly milled pepper and only a very little salt—because of the bacon. Now beat the remaining egg with the milk and pour it over the contents of the pie. Then roll out the rest of the pastry to make a lid, dampen the edges and seal well. Decorate with any trimmings, make a small hole in the centre and brush the top with milk. Place the pie on the baking sheet on a highish shelf in the oven and bake for 10 minutes; then reduce the heat to mark 4/350 °F and bake for a further 30 minutes. This pie is very good eaten cold and is ideal picnic food.

Cheese Soufflé

(Serves 3–4)

This is always a good standby recipe for using up old bits of cheese that lurk in the bottom of the fridge.

3 oz grated cheese
3 large eggs, separated
1 oz plain flour
1 oz butter
¼ pint milk
2 pinches cayenne pepper
½ teaspoon dried mustard
A few gratings of nutmeg
Salt and freshly milled black pepper
A little extra butter

Pre-heat the oven to mark 5/375 °F

Well butter a 1½-pint soufflé dish (or a pie dish). Then take a medium-sized saucepan, melt 1 oz butter in it, add the flour and stir it over a medium heat for 2 minutes. Now add the milk gradually, stirring all the time till you have a smooth paste, and cook it very gently for 3 minutes (still stirring). Next stir in the mustard, cayenne, nutmeg, salt and pepper, and allow the sauce to cool a bit before stirring in the grated cheese, followed by the egg yolks—which should be beaten quite thoroughly first. Now whisk the egg whites till stiff, beat a couple of dollops into the sauce, then fold the rest in very carefully and gently, so as not to lose all the air you've beaten into them. Pile the mixture into the soufflé dish next, then place it on a baking sheet in the centre of the oven for about 30 35 minutes. To test if the soufflé is cooked, push a skewer down into the centre—if it comes out clean and doesn't look too liquid, it's cooked.

Poached Eggs with Spinach Soufflé

A very impressive way to serve eggs and spinach.

2 lb fresh spinach
4 fresh eggs
2 oz butter
2 oz flour
½ pint milk
2 oz grated cheese
3 egg yolks
4 egg whites
Freshly grated nutmeg
Some more butter
Dry white breadcrumbs
Salt and freshly milled black pepper

Pre-heat the oven to mark 5/375 °F with a baking sheet in it

First of all liberally butter a soufflé dish (7 inches in diameter) and dust the inside of the dish evenly with a few dry white breadcrumbs. Then thoroughly wash the spinach in several changes of cold water and pick it over, removing any thick, tough stalks or damaged leaves. Next press the leaves into a large saucepan, sprinkle with 2 teaspoons of salt (but don't add water), cover and cook for 7–10 minutes. Then drain the spinach thoroughly in a colander and chop it fairly finely. Now melt 2 oz butter in a medium-sized saucepan and stir in the flour. Cook for a minute or two before gradually stirring in the milk. Bring to boiling point and simmer, still stirring, for about 1 minute before removing the pan from the heat. Then beat the chopped spinach and two-thirds of the cheese into the mixture with the egg yolks. Now taste and season with salt, pepper and a generous amount of nutmeg. At this stage *lightly* poach 4 eggs for 3 minutes in a frying pan of barely simmering water. While they're poaching, beat the egg whites till stiff, fold them carefully into the spinach mixture, then pour half the soufflé mixture into the dish, add the poached eggs (well drained), cover with the rest of the soufflé mixture and sprinkle the top with the remaining cheese. Bake on the baking sheet for 30–35 minutes, or until it is well risen and browned on top.

Cauliflower, Egg and Celery au Gratin (Serves 3–4)

This is a good one for vegetarians or anyone else who wants a delicious meal without any meat.

1 head English celery
1 cauliflower
2 hardboiled eggs, quartered
¼ lb mushrooms, sliced
1 large onion, peeled and chopped
2 oz butter
2 oz flour
½ pint milk
3 oz grated Cheddar cheese
1 tablespoon dried breadcrumbs
1 bayleaf
¼ whole nutmeg, grated
Salt and freshly milled black pepper
2 pinches cayenne pepper
A little extra butter

Pre-heat the oven to mark 7/425°F

Scrub and chop the celery into chunks and cook it in a little boiling salted water for about 20 minutes. The cauliflower needs to be trimmed, washed and sat in about 1 inch of boiling salted water, together with the bayleaf, for about 10–15 minutes with the lid on the saucepan (both the celery and the cauliflower should be tender but still firm). When the cauliflower is ready, drain it—reserving the water—then separate it into small florets and arrange them in a buttered fireproof dish along with the celery, sliced mushrooms and the quarters of hardboiled egg. Now make the sauce by gently cooking the chopped onion in 2 oz of butter for about 10 minutes, then stirring in the flour and adding the milk bit by bit, stirring all the time. When all the milk is in, add $\frac{1}{4}-\frac{1}{2}$ pint of cauliflower water in the same way till you have a smooth sauce. Cook it gently for 6 minutes, then taste it, add salt and pepper and about $\frac{1}{4}$ of a whole nutmeg, grated. Pour the sauce over the vegetables, sprinkle the grated cheese over, then the breadcrumbs, dot with flecks of butter and bake on a high shelf for 10 minutes until the cheese has browned and melted. Sprinkle with a couple of pinches of cayenne and serve hot.

Egg and Anchovy Salad

(Serves 4)

This is a nice dish for lunch on a hot summer's day with, maybe, a cold soup to start with.

1 lb new potatoes (cooked)
$\frac{1}{4}$ lb cooked French beans (or sliced runner beans)
6 eggs
A 2-oz tin anchovy fillets, well drained
Salt and freshly milled black pepper
1 quantity of vinaigrette dressing with herbs (see p. 143)

To finish:
1 lettuce, cleaned and prepared
1 oz black olives

Put the eggs in a saucepan, cover them with cold water, bring them up to a gentle simmer and cook gently for exactly 7 minutes. Then cool them rapidly under cold running water until they're quite cold. Now take the shells off and chop the eggs roughly, seasoning them with a little salt and pepper. Then slice the potatoes into rounds and cut the beans into 1-inch lengths. Now take a large bowl, carefully mix the chopped eggs, beans and potatoes together, and pour in nearly all the vinaigrette dressing, keeping a little for later. Stir again, to get everything coated with the dressing, then cover the mixture and chill it until needed. To serve the salad, arrange the lettuce leaves in a salad bowl and sprinkle them with the reserved dressing; then arrange the potato mixture over the lettuce, make a criss-cross pattern with the anchovies and finally sprinkle on the black olives.

Potato and Cheese Baked Eggs (Serves 2)

This is a fairly economical supper dish that tastes especially good with homemade tomato sauce.

2 lb potatoes
A 5-oz carton soured cream
3 oz butter
6 oz grated Cheddar cheese
Salt and freshly milled black pepper
4 large fresh eggs
A little extra butter
A few chopped chives or spring onion tops

Pre-heat the oven to mark 5/375 °F

Peel the potatoes, place them in a saucepan with some salt, pour boiling water on to them and cook them for about 25 minutes, or until tender. Then drain them, add the 3 oz of butter and the soured cream, start to mash them with a fork and finish off by whipping them to a purée with an electric mixer. Now add the cheese, taste and season with salt and pepper. Next butter a shallow ovenproof baking dish, arrange the potato mixture in the dish and, with the back of a tablespoon, make 4 depressions. Now break an egg carefully into each depression, place the dish in the oven and bake for 15 minutes, or until the eggs are just set. Serve sprinkled with chopped chives or spring onion tops.

Eggs Savoyard

For this recipe for 4 people you could use 4 individual oven-proof bowls (about ½ pint capacity), but failing that you can cook the whole lot in a large gratin dish.

1 lb potatoes, peeled
2 oz butter
1 onion, peeled and finely chopped
4 eggs
8 tablespoons single cream
4 oz grated Cheddar cheese
Salt and freshly milled black pepper

Pre-heat the oven to mark 6/400 °F

First of all place the potatoes in a saucepan with some salt, pour in some boiling water and cook them for about 25 minutes. Then drain them, slice the potatoes (as you would for frying) and arrange an equal quantity in the base of each bowl. Next heat the butter in a saucepan and fry the onion until softened and golden. Then spoon a little of the melted butter and onion mixture over the sliced potatoes in each dish, and season with freshly milled pepper and salt. Now make a slight depression in each bowl and carefully break in an egg. Next spoon 2 tablespoons of cream over each egg and season again with salt and pepper. Then sprinkle with cheese and bake in the oven for 15–20 minutes, or until hot and bubbling with the yolk still fairly soft. Serve absolutely immediately.

Bacon, Leek and Potato Omelette

(Serves 2)

This is a flat omelette, finished off under the grill, so it shouldn't be folded—just simply cut in half or in quarters.

2 tablespoons oil
2 potatoes
1 leek
4 oz streaky bacon, rinded and diced
4 large eggs
A generous pinch mixed herbs
Salt and freshly milled black pepper

Peel and dice the potatoes and dry them on some kitchen paper; then trim the leek top and bottom. Slice it in half first lengthways and then across into $\frac{1}{4}$-inch thick strips, wash carefully in plenty of cold water, and drain and dry thoroughly. In a frying pan, about 6 inches in diameter, heat the oil and add the diced potato. Cook gently for about 10 minutes, stirring frequently. When the potato is just tender, add the chopped leek and diced bacon to the pan. Stir well, cover with a suitably sized lid and cook over a low heat for a further 5–8 minutes. Meanwhile break the eggs into a bowl. Season well with salt, freshly milled pepper and mixed herbs. Stir to blend the eggs together, then pour the mixture over the contents of the pan. Shake the pan and cook over a low heat until the underside of the omelette is cooked and lightly golden. Meanwhile pre-heat the grill, then transfer the pan to the grill and continue to cook gently until the egg on the surface is just set. Cut the omelette in half or quarters and serve on warmed plates. This is nice with a crisp salad.

Spanish Tortilla

(Serves 2)

Tortilla, or Spanish omelette, can sometimes be just a mish-mash of leftovers incorporated in an omelette—but this is a real one made with green peppers and Spanish chorizo sausage.

4 large eggs
2 potatoes, peeled and diced
1 small green pepper, de-seeded and chopped
1 medium onion, peeled and chopped
A 2-oz piece Spanish chorizo sausage, also chopped small
3 tablespoons oil
Salt and freshly milled black pepper

For this you need a thick, heavy, medium-sized frying pan. Put 2 tablespoons of oil in it, then add the diced potatoes and cook them gently for about 8–10 minutes, stirring them around so that they brown evenly. Next add the onion, pepper and chorizo, stir again and continue cooking for a further 8–10 minutes, or until the potato and onion are soft. Now break the eggs into a bowl, season them well, beat them just a little bit with a fork, then pour them into the pan and, keeping the heat at medium, cook for 2 or 3 minutes, shaking the pan from time to time to prevent the eggs from sticking. When the omelette is firm but still slightly moist, slide it out on to a plate, then quickly heat the other tablespoon of oil in the pan and slide the omelette back in on its other side. Cook for another 3 minutes and serve cut in wedges.

Note: Chorizo sausage is available at delicatessen and special-ised food shops.

Omelette Piperade   (Serves 2)

Another quick supper dish for 2 people; good towards the end
of the summer when the tomatoes are plentiful and green
peppers are cheap.

For 2 omelettes the ingredients are:

Oil or butter
1 large green pepper, de-seeded and chopped
½ lb ripe tomatoes, skinned and chopped
1 onion, peeled and chopped
1 clove garlic, crushed
½ teaspoon dried basil
4 eggs
Salt and freshly milled black pepper

Heat a little oil in a medium-sized pan, then stir in the chopped
pepper, chopped onion and crushed garlic, and cook over a
medium heat for about 5 minutes. Then add the tomatoes and
dried basil, season with salt and freshly milled black pepper,
and cook gently without a cover for about 20 minutes. Now get
ready for the first omelette by breaking 2 eggs into a bowl,
seasoning with salt and pepper and stirring lightly with a fork.
Then heat a smear of oil in an omelette pan and, when it is
really hot, pour in the beaten egg and start to draw the eggs
in to cook the omelette. After a few seconds, spoon half the
pepper and tomato mixture over half the omelette, fold the
other half of the omelette over the filling and invert the pan to
tip the omelette out on to a warmed plate. Now quickly
prepare the other omelette, using the remaining filling, and
serve immediately with some crusty bread and a nice crisp
green salad.

Frugal Fish

The funny thing is, frugal fish is usually the freshest. The more
expensive deep-sea fish, like cod and haddock, are very often
three weeks old before they're landed—and (in my opinion)
their dull flavour shows it. Since our home-caught herring and

mackerel have far more character and flavour, I wonder why it's necessary to go off and fight wars over dull old cod?

But then we are a nation of fish-finger addicts, and once you've bitten your way through the bright orange bread-crumbs, what you've got is probably cod. We've already spoken of convenience versus cost but, quite honestly, fish fingers are outrageously expensive (I once reckoned up the price per pound of frozen fish fingers and discovered that in the same supermarket frozen rainbow trout was actually cheaper, and as it happens every bit as convenient but without the nasty breadcrumbs).

In this chapter I'm hoping to lure you on to a few very delicious recipes for herring and mackerel. I think it's a pity that because they were once less than a halfpenny each they've always had a poverty-stricken reputation. Well, when it comes to shopping for food we're all pretty poor now, so here's to their comeback! In the other recipes in this chapter I've attempted to make a little fish go a long way.

Also, when a recipe calls for white fish, do try the lesser-known varieties like pollack or red fish (sometimes called Norwegian cod) which are usually half the price of cod or haddock—and for any sort of fish pie, coley is very good.

Whiting au Gratin

(Serves 4)

2 lb whiting (ask the fishmonger to fillet and skin it for you)
4 oz mushrooms, thinly sliced
1 oz butter
1 onion, peeled, halved and thinly sliced
1 teaspoon lemon juice
3 fl. oz dry cider
4 tablespoons dry white breadcrumbs
2 tablespoons grated cheese
A little extra butter
Salt and freshly milled black pepper

Pre-heat the oven to mark 4/350 °F

First heat the 1 oz of butter in a saucepan and fry the onions gently until softened (about 10 minutes). Then stir in the mushrooms and lemon juice, and cook for about 3–4 minutes more. Season with salt and pepper, then spread the mixture over the base of a buttered gratin dish. Lay the wiped fillets on top and season again with salt and pepper. Next pour in just enough cider to cover the mushroom/onion base. Finally sprinkle the breadcrumbs and cheese all over, dot with flecks of butter and bake—uncovered—on a high shelf in the oven for 25 minutes.

Old Fashioned Soused Herrings

(Serves 3)

Homemade rollmops beat anything that ever came out of a jar.

6 herrings
6 teaspoons made mustard
2 dill pickles, sliced lengthways into 3
1 large onion, peeled and thinly sliced into rings
½ pint cider vinegar
¼ pint dry cider
¾ pint water
3 juniper berries
3 allspice berries
2 cloves
8 peppercorns
1 bayleaf

Pre-heat the oven to mark 4/350 °F

You will need a shallow baking dish or casserole for this and also 6 toothpicks.

Ask the fishmonger to head, gut and fillet the herrings but to leave their tails on. When you get them home, check that all the bones have been removed and wipe the fillets as dry as possible with some kitchen paper. Now spread the filleted side of each fish with a teaspoon of mustard and place a slice of dill pickle across what was the head end of each fillet. Sprinkle the rest with some of the separated onion rings, roll up each fillet from the head end to the tail, being careful to get them as tight and neat as possible, and secure with a toothpick (through the tail end and out the other side). Now pack the rolls fairly tightly into the baking dish or casserole. Then prepare the marinade by placing the vinegar, cider and ¾ pint of water in a saucepan, together with the herbs and spices. Bring the liquid to the boil and simmer (uncovered) for 10 minutes. Then take the pan from the heat and leave until the liquid is cold. To cook the herrings, pour the cold marinade over, cover with a lid or double foil and bake in the centre of the oven for 15 minutes. When they're cooked, let them get quite cold in the liquid, then cover them and put them in the refrigerator for at least 48 hours before serving. Serve, if possible, with rye bread.

Herrings Fried in Oatmeal (Serves 2)

Just the thing for 'high tea' with some brown bread and butter and freshly made tea.

4 herrings, gutted
3 tablespoons medium oatmeal
2 oz lard
Salt and freshly milled black pepper

First gut the herrings as described on p. 54. Then heat the lard in a large frying pan and, while it's heating, wipe the herrings with kitchen paper to get them as dry as possible. Season the oatmeal with freshly ground black pepper and salt, and then coat the herrings in it, pressing it down all over quite firmly. When the fat is hot and sizzling, fry the herrings in it for approximately 4 minutes on each side, until they're crisp and golden. Then drain them on crumpled greaseproof paper and serve with wedges of lemon to squeeze over them. Powdered mustard mixed with cream (or top of the milk) goes very well with this dish and, instead of bread and butter, plain boiled potatoes.

Baked Fish Soufflé

(Serves 4)

12 ounces of whiting fillets, or any white fish, is instantly made more special by making it into a fluffy soufflé.

12 oz whiting fillets (cooked in ½ pint of milk then strained—with the milk reserved)
2 oz butter
1½ oz flour
4 egg yolks
5 egg whites
2 tablespoons grated Parmesan
2 teaspoons lemon juice
1 tablespoon finely chopped parsley
1 teaspoon anchovy essence
3 spring onions, finely sliced
Salt and cayenne pepper

Pre-heat the oven to mark 6/400 °F

Flake the fish, discarding the skin and bones as you go, then put it on one side whilst you make a sauce by melting the butter in a saucepan then stirring in the flour. Cook this for a minute or two before gradually adding the strained milk. Bring to the boil, stirring, and boil gently for 1 minute. Then remove the pan from the heat and beat in the egg yolks, 1 tablespoon of Parmesan, the lemon juice, parsley, anchovy essence, spring onions and the fish. Season well with salt and ½ teaspoon of cayenne pepper. Next whisk the egg whites to the stiff peak stage. Then fold them into the fish mixture, taste and season again if necessary. Now pour the mixture into a buttered 3-pint soufflé dish or deep baking dish, and sprinkle with the remaining Parmesan cheese. Transfer the soufflé to the oven, placing it on a baking sheet, and turn down the heat immediately to mark 5/375 °F. Cook for 35–40 minutes, or until the soufflé is well risen and golden brown, then serve absolutely immediately.

Baked Fish with Potatoes and Anchovies

(Serves 3)

Any white fish can be used for this, because there's lots of flavour added.

1 lb potatoes, peeled and very thinly sliced
1 lb white fish, skinned
1 onion, peeled and finely chopped
¼ pint milk
6 tablespoons chopped parsley
1 clove garlic, crushed
Finely grated rind of 1 lemon
6 anchovy fillets, finely chopped
1 oz butter
Salt and freshly milled black pepper

Pre-heat the oven to mark 4/350 °F

Put a layer of potato slices in the base of a deepish, well-buttered baking dish and sprinkle with half the finely chopped onion. Then mix the parsley, garlic, lemon rind and finely chopped anchovy fillets together and sprinkle a little of this mixture in the dish before adding another layer of potatoes, some onion and another sprinkling of parsley mixture. Finish off with a final layer of potatoes (reserving a little of the parsley mixture). Now bring the milk up to the boil, season with a little salt and plenty of pepper, then pour this over the potatoes, fleck the top with butter and bake (uncovered) for 40 minutes. Meanwhile cut the fish into smallish cubes; then after the 40 minutes is up, put the fish on top of the potatoes and sprinkle with the remaining parsley mixture and a few more flecks of butter, and bake for a further 15 minutes, or until the fish is cooked.

Mackerels en Papillote

Cooking mackerel in paper cases keeps the flesh beautifully moist and tender.

2 mackerels, headed and gutted
2 oz butter
4 tablespoons finely chopped parsley
1 small onion, peeled and grated
1 clove garlic, crushed
Juice of 1 lemon
¼ teaspoon dried tarragon
A generous pinch cayenne pepper
1½ oz butter (melted)
Salt and freshly milled black pepper

Pre-heat the oven to mark 6/400 °F

Wipe the fish as dry as possible with kitchen paper, inside and out, and season them with salt and freshly milled black pepper. Then mix the 2 oz of butter with the parsley, onion, garlic, lemon juice, tarragon and cayenne pepper and beat everything thoroughly to blend well. Then spread an equal quantity inside each fish. Now take two large circles of double thickness greaseproof paper (each large enough to take a fish comfortably) and brush them with the melted butter. Then lay each fish in the middle on the buttered side, and wrap one side of the paper circle over the fish (to make a sort of Cornish pasty shape). Secure the edges by pinching them together, making small folds, then pop both parcels on to a baking sheet and bake for 30 minutes. Unwrap and serve with the juice from the packets poured over.

Mackerel with Rhubarb Sauce   (Serves 2)

Not quite so famous as mackerel with gooseberries but just as good—the acidic fruit counteracts the richness of the fish perfectly.

2 mackerel, gutted (ask the fishmonger to do this for you)
½ lb rhubarb
1 level tablespoon demerara sugar
½ level teaspoon ground ginger
¼ pint water
Salt and freshly milled black pepper

Make the sauce first by chopping the rhubarb into smallish chunks and putting it into a thick-based saucepan, adding the sugar, ginger and water. Then put a lid on and let it cook over a fairly gentle heat, shaking the saucepan from time to time. It will probably take around 15–20 minutes to soften. Now rub the contents of the saucepan through a sieve, or purée it in an electric blender, and taste to check that there is enough sugar (although it should be a fairly sharp sauce). Now pre-heat the grill, wipe the mackerel as dry as possible with kitchen paper, season the insides of the fish, then make three diagonal slashes across the backbone of each fish and grill them for about 4–6 minutes on each side. While they're grilling, re-heat the sauce and serve it with the fish, together with new potatoes.

Fish Cakes with Capers

(Serves 4–6)

A good way to make a pound of fish seem just like 2 pounds.

1 lb creamed, mashed potatoes
1 lb poached cod (well drained)
2 tablespoons chopped parsley
¾ teaspoon anchovy essence
1 heaped teaspoon capers, chopped
1 egg, beaten
1 oz butter
1 teaspoon lemon juice
Some grated nutmeg
1 clove garlic, crushed
Salt and freshly milled black pepper
A generous pinch cayenne pepper
Flour

For the coating:
2 eggs, beaten
6 oz (approx.) dry white breadcrumbs

Take a large mixing bowl and thoroughly combine all the ingredients (except those for the coating) together; then taste, adding salt and pepper and a pinch of cayenne. (If the fish and potatoes are not freshly cooked and hot, the butter will need to be melted before adding it to the mixture.) Now cool and chill the mixture for an hour or two to get it nice and firm, then when you're ready to cook the fish cakes, lightly flour a working surface, turn the fish mixture out on to it and form it into a long roll about 2–2½ inches in diameter. Cut the roll into 12 round fish cakes. Pat each cake into a neat shape, and dip each one first into beaten egg and then in the dry white breadcrumbs. Now shallow fry the cakes in equal quantities of oil and butter until golden brown on both sides. Drain on crumpled kitchen paper and serve inmediately. Tartare sauce or fresh parsley sauce would be a nice accompaniment.

Deep Fried Sprats with Mustard Sauce

(Serves 2)

Sprats are smaller cousins belonging to the herring family. In the good old days when herrings were cheap and humble, sprats were even humbler and it's only now that they're coming into their own again, which is a good thing because they are delicious.

1 lb sprats
Some seasoned flour
Groundnut oil for frying

For the Mustard Sauce:
1 oz butter
½ oz flour
½ pint milk
½ small onion, peeled and chopped
2 teaspoons dry mustard
Salt and freshly milled black pepper
2 teaspoons lemon juice
A generous pinch sugar
2 pinches cayenne pepper

Begin by making the mustard sauce. In a saucepan melt the butter and soften the chopped onion in it for about 10 minutes. Then stir in the flour, and let it cook very gently for a couple of minutes before mixing in the mustard powder. Next add the milk bit by bit, stirring constantly. When all the milk is in, bring the sauce to the boil and let it simmer very gently for about 3 minutes. Then season to taste with salt, freshly milled black pepper, lemon juice and a pinch of sugar. Now keep the sauce warm whilst you gut and cook the sprats.

Make a small incision behind a gill of each fish and gently squeeze the belly up towards the head to gut the fish, at the same time trying to leave the head intact. Then rinse the fish well and dry them thoroughly on some kitchen paper before tossing in seasoned flour. Next heat a deep pan of oil to 360 °F or, if you don't have a thermometer, until a small cube of bread dropped into it turns golden and crisp in 1 minute. Then fry the sprats in the oil for about 3 minutes. You will probably need to fry them in at least 2 batches. Then drain on crumpled greaseproof paper, keeping them hot, and serve as soon as possible sprinkled with a trace of cayenne and with the mustard sauce poured over.

Herrings with Caper Stuffing (Serves 4)

4 herrings, gutted and boned

For the stuffing:
1 medium onion, peeled and chopped small
3 oz fresh white breadcrumbs
1 oz butter
1 teaspoon mustard powder
Zest of 1 lemon, finely grated
Juice of ½ lemon
3 tablespoons finely chopped parsley
1 tablespoon drained capers, chopped
An extra 1 oz butter
Salt and freshly milled black pepper

Pre-heat the oven to mark 7/425°F

To make the stuffing, first mix the breadcrumbs, mustard powder, parsley, lemon rind and juice, and capers together in a large mixing bowl. Now heat 1 oz of butter in a frying pan and soften the onion in it for 10 minutes, before adding it (together with its buttery juices) to the breadcrumbs mixture and seasoning everything with salt and freshly milled pepper.

Now open each herring out flat, and spread a quarter of the stuffing down one side of each one, then fold the other side back to its original shape. Put the fish in a well-buttered shallow baking dish (or else a roasting tin lined with foil), place a knob of butter on each one and bake near the top of the oven for 15 minutes, basting once with the buttery juices.

Kipper Quiche   (Serves 4 as a main course)

A less frugal version of this can be made for a special occasion
by substituting ½ pint cream for the milk.

6 oz shortcrust pastry (see p. 40)
A pair of kippers (about 12 oz)
A squeeze of lemon juice
½ pint milk
2 large eggs
2 teaspoons French mustard
Freshly grated nutmeg
Salt and freshly milled black pepper
A generous pinch cayenne pepper

Pre-heat the oven to mark 4/350 °F with a baking sheet in it

Grill the kippers for a few minutes on each side, then set them
aside to cool. Meanwhile make the pastry and line a 9–9½-inch
fluted flan tin with it. Prick it all over the base with a fork and
bake on the baking sheet near the top of the oven for 10
minutes, then remove the flan and increase the temperature of
the oven to mark 5/375 °F. Next carefully skin the fish,
separate the flesh into large flakes, lay these over the base of
the pastry case and squeeze a little lemon juice over the top.
Now whisk the milk, eggs, mustard and freshly grated nutmeg
together with some salt and pepper. Place the flan on the heated
baking sheet in the centre of the oven, pour the liquid
mixture carefully into it and sprinkle with cayenne pepper.
Then bake for about 40 minutes until the filling is slightly
puffed and golden. Served hot, warm or cold, it is delicious.

Salmon Fish Cakes (Serves 3)

I think tinned salmon makes very good fish cakes, as nice as if you'd used fresh.

A 7½-oz tin salmon
½ lb potatoes, peeled
2 tablespoons chopped parsley
2 gherkins, finely chopped
2 hardboiled eggs, chopped
2 teaspoons lemon juice
1 teaspoon anchovy essence
Flour
Equal parts of oil and butter for frying
Salt and freshly milled black pepper
A good pinch cayenne pepper

Begin by boiling the potatoes in salted water, then drain and mash them. Meanwhile drain the liquor from the salmon, discarding any skin or bones, and mash it to a paste with a fork. Then combine the potato with the fish, parsley, gherkins, hardboiled egg, lemon juice and anchovy essence. Mix everything thoroughly, taste and season with salt, freshly milled black pepper and cayenne. Next form the mixture into 6 fish cakes and dust each one with flour (all this can be done in advance). Then fry the fish cakes in the hot fat on both sides until golden. Drain and serve hot, garnished with sprigs of parsley and wedges of lemon.

Cold Marinaded Mackerel (Serves 2)

This makes a lovely summer dish to serve on a very hot day with, perhaps, some rice salad to accompany it.

2 good-sized fresh mackerel
½ lb ripe tomatoes, skinned, de-seeded and chopped
1 small green pepper, de-seeded and finely chopped
1 small onion, peeled and finely chopped
½ small lemon, thinly sliced
¼ pint dry cider
3 tablespoons cider vinegar
4 tablespoons oil
½ teaspoon mixed herbs
2 level tablespoons chopped fresh parsley
Salt and freshly milled black pepper
2 pinches cayenne pepper

Have the fishmonger gut the mackerel for you, leaving the heads on. Wipe them clean with kitchen paper, then arrange the fish in an oval fireproof casserole just large enough to hold them side by side—alternatively, you could fit them into a frying pan. Now place the rest of the ingredients (except the parsley) in a saucepan, cover and simmer for 20 minutes. Taste, season with salt, freshly milled black pepper and a couple of pinches of cayenne, then pour the mixture over the fish in the casserole. Now bring it up to the boil and simmer very gently for just 5 minutes. Turn the fish over very carefully, cover again and leave them to become quite cold in the juices in the casserole. Serve sprinkled with chopped fresh parsley.

Mackerel with Caper Sauce (Serves 2)

2 fresh mackerel, headed and gutted (get the fishmonger to do
  this for you)
5 tablespoons oil
1 large clove garlic, crushed
4 oz capers, drained and coarsely crushed
Juice of 1 large lemon
Salt and freshly milled black pepper

A few hours before you need to cook the fish, put the oil in a
bowl with the crushed garlic and beat in the lemon juice,
followed by the capers and some salt and pepper. Then leave
it on one side for the flavours to develop. When you are ready
to cook the fish, remove the grill rack from the grill and line it
with foil. Pre-heat the grill and arrange the fish on the foil,
after gashing each side of the fish twice (in the thickest part of
their bodies). Sprinkle with salt and pepper, and pour the
caper sauce in and around the fish. Brush a little oil over each
one. Grill under a high heat so that the skins turn crisply
brown—they will need 3–4 minutes on each side. Then serve
with all the pan juices poured over. You'll need lots of crusty
bread to mop up the juices.

Tomato and Anchovy Quiche (Serves 4 as a main course)

This has a lovely Mediterranean flavour and tastes very good
eaten out of doors on a hot summer's day.

Shortcrust pastry (made with 6 oz flour and 3 oz fat—see p. 40)
1 tablespoon olive oil
2 medium onions, peeled and finely chopped
1 clove garlic, crushed
1½ lb tomatoes, skinned, de-seeded and chopped
1 teaspoon dried basil
1 small tin anchovy fillets
3 tablespoons tomato purée
2 tablespoons chopped parsley

2 eggs
1 oz black olives, pitted and halved
2 tablespoons grated Parmesan cheese
Salt and freshly milled black pepper

Pre-heat the oven to mark 4/350 °F

Begin by lining a 10-inch flan tin with the pastry, prick the base all over with a fork and pre-cook it on a baking sheet for 15 minutes. Then remove it from the oven and increase the heat to mark 5/375 °F. Meanwhile heat the oil in a medium-sized saucepan and cook the finely chopped onion and crushed garlic over a gentle heat until softened but not coloured. Then stir in the chopped tomatoes and basil, and cook, uncovered, over a fairly high heat until the mixture is reduced to a thick consistency and most of the excess liquid has evaporated. Now drain the anchovies, retaining the oil from the can. Chop up 6 anchovies, then cut the rest in half lengthways and keep them on one side. Remove the pan from the heat and stir in the 6 chopped fillets, tomato purée and parsley; then beat the eggs together in a basin before stirring them into the tomato mixture. Taste and season with pepper and a little salt if it needs it. Now spread the mixture evenly in the pre-cooked flan case and decorate the top with a lattice-work of the remaining halved anchovy fillets. Then sprinkle over the pitted, halved black olives. Sprinkle the surface with the oil retained from the anchovy can and finally with the Parmesan cheese. Now bake for 40 minutes until the filling is puffed and is a light brown.

CHICKENS LIB

Chicken is a problem. The cheapest form of chicken is the frozen variety, and 80 per cent of all chickens sold in this country are frozen: being only 7 8 weeks old, they are also tasteless, and have probably been fed on fish protein (which has an alarming knack of impregnating a bird with a fishy flavour if not removed from the diet a month before the bird is killed). On the other hand, the best chicken to buy is the one that has been allowed to hang in the family butcher's and is drawn only at the point of purchase, but that is also the most expensive.

It's not quite as straightforward as that, though. Very many frozen chickens that come off the production line are eviscerated quickly, then plunged into a trough of iced water to be cooled rapidly. At the same time they absorb up to 10 per cent of their own weight in water and then are packed off to be frozen, water and all. You are in effect paying for 10 per cent water when you buy many frozen chickens.

Fortunately, there is an alternative to water-cooling, and that is air-cooling (a method pioneered by Marks & Spencer), in which no water is absorbed to increase weight or extract flavour. That is why their fresh-chilled chickens don't have the bleached white look which so many mass-produced varieties have: they have that healthy pinkish tinge you find on fresh chickens hanging in butchers.

In short, if you can't get hold of a freshly drawn bird from a butcher, my advice is to plump for a Marks & Spencer air-chilled chicken—and in the interests of frugality, go back to the days when chicken was a *treat* by having fewer but better-flavoured ones. You can always make up the shortfall by having rabbit once in a while—now there's a neglected delicacy.

Chicken Pot Roast

(Serves 4–6)

Needless to say you'll need a freshly drawn chicken for this, and ask your supplier to be sure to give you the giblets.

A 3½-lb roasting chicken
1 largish onion, peeled and stuck with 3 cloves
4 leeks, trimmed and washed
4 carrots, scraped
4 sticks celery, halved
A few parsley stalks
1 bayleaf
1 clove garlic, crushed
Butter
Salt and freshly milled black pepper

Pre-heat the oven to mark 8/450 °F

First rub the inside of the chicken with salt and pepper and a little butter. Then place the onion stuck with cloves inside the chicken and rub some butter and seasoning over the outside. Now put the chicken in a roasting tin and bake in the top half of the oven for about 30 minutes, by which time it should have developed a nice golden brown skin. Then remove it from the oven and transfer it, together with any juices, to a deep pot. Surround the chicken with the vegetables, herbs and garlic, and pour over sufficient water to not quite cover the bird, adding the giblets as well. Bring to boiling point and simmer very gently with the lid on for about 1 hour, or until the chicken is tender. Then remove the chicken and cut it into 4 portions; place the portions on a warmed serving dish surrounded by the vegetables, cover and keep warm. Now discard the giblets and boil the remaining stock briskly until it has reduced and the flavour has concentrated. Spoon some of the juices over the chicken and vegetables, sprinkle with chopped parsley and serve. Any stock left over can be used for soup.

Poulet à la Catalane   (Serves 6)

This is a good recipe if you're looking for an inexpensive dish
for a special occasion, especially in the autumn when peppers
and aubergines are at their cheapest.

1 fresh chicken (about 3½–4 lb) cut into 6 joints
2 oz butter
Olive oil
8 fl. oz dry cider
2 medium onions, peeled and chopped
1 clove garlic, crushed
3 small aubergines, cut into 1-inch cubes
2 medium green peppers, de-seeded and sliced
¼ lb mushrooms, sliced
6 tomatoes, skinned, chopped and sliced
1 sprig fresh thyme
1 bayleaf
4 oz Spanish stuffed olives, sliced
Salt and freshly milled black pepper

Pre-heat the oven to mark 5/375 °F

In a large flameproof casserole heat the butter and 2 tablespoons
of the oil together. Season the chicken joints and cook them to
a nice golden brown, turning them over in the hot fat, then
add the onions and the crushed garlic. Stir them around and
let them cook for about 5–7 minutes. Now pour in the cider,
let it bubble for a minute or two, add the thyme and bayleaf,
then put the lid on and place the casserole in the oven to cook
for about 45 minutes. Towards the end of that time, heat a
little more of the oil in a frying pan and gently cook the
chopped aubergines, peppers, tomatoes and mushrooms till
soft, seasoning well with salt and freshly milled pepper. When
the chicken is ready, take the casserole out of the oven, add
all the vegetables plus the sliced olives and simmer the whole
lot on top of the stove for about 5 minutes. Then spoon off any
surplus fat, extract the thyme and bayleaf, and serve the chicken
on a warmed serving dish, garnished if you like with little
triangular croutons of crisp-fried bread.

Devilled Chicken Drumsticks (Serves 3)

If you have a Marks & Spencer in your area, they do very reasonably priced packets of chicken drumsticks.

6 chicken drumsticks
2 tablespoons Worcestershire sauce
1 tablespoon tomato paste
1 tablespoon tomato ketchup
1 teaspoon made English mustard
1 teaspoon French mustard
1 teaspoon sugar
1 teaspoon soy sauce
1 teaspoon paprika
1 tablespoon oil
Salt and freshly milled black pepper

Start by arranging the chicken drumsticks in a single layer in the grill pan with the grid removed; then, using a skewer, stab the joints in several places. Now in a mixing bowl combine all the remaining ingredients together and stir thoroughly until smooth. Pour this mixture over the chicken and turn the pieces around in it. Then leave it, covered with foil, in a cool place for a minimum of 3 hours—or much longer if you like. To cook, pre-heat the grill, and then grill the chicken for about 15-20 minutes, or until the drumsticks are cooked. Keep turning them fairly frequently to prevent them burning, and serve very hot with any pan juices spooned over.

Pilau rice cooked with chopped onion and green pepper (see p. 157) is nice with this.

Chicken and Chick Peas (Serves 4)

Chick peas (available at wholefood shops) give an unusual flavour to a chicken casserole as well as making it more substantial, but they do need a long soaking beforehand.

A 2½–3-lb roasting chicken, quartered
½ lb chick peas, soaked overnight
1 large onion, peeled, halved and sliced
2 cloves garlic, crushed
1 oz butter
2 tablespoons oil
A 14-oz can Italian tomatoes
1 teaspoon dried basil
1 bayleaf
1–2 tablespoons tomato purée
½ pint stock (made from the giblets)
Salt and freshly milled black pepper

Pre-heat the oven to mark 3/325 °F

To start with, the soaked chick peas should be placed in a saucepan with enough fresh water to cover them to a depth of about 2 inches, then brought to the boil. Simmer (uncovered) for about 30 minutes, skimming after about 10 minutes—and don't bother to add any salt at this stage. While that's happening, heat the butter and oil together in a flameproof casserole, then dry the chicken quarters on kitchen paper and fry in the hot fat over a medium heat until they're evenly browned. Then, using a draining spoon, remove them to a plate and in the fat remaining in the pan gently fry the sliced onion and crushed garlic until softened. Now return the chicken joints to the pan and pour over the contents of the can of tomatoes and the chicken stock. Then drain the cooked chick peas, reserving their cooking liquor. Now add them to the chicken mixture, with ¼ pint of the cooking liquor as well. Next add the bayleaf, tomato purée and basil, and season with a little salt and pepper. Bring up to simmering point, cover and transfer the casserole to the oven. Bake for 30 minutes, then remove the lid and bake for a further 30 minutes. Taste the juices and add a bit more seasoning, if necessary, before serving. This dish is nice served with rice flavoured with onion.

Southern Fried Chicken (Serves 4)

I use the packets of chicken thighs or drumsticks for this, but you could use a 3-lb chicken cut in 8 pieces.

8 chicken joints
A little milk
4 oz plain flour
½ teaspoon baking powder
Groundnut oil for deep frying
Salt and freshly milled black pepper

Into a wide, deep pan pour enough oil to give a depth of 1 inch and heat to 350 °F, or until a small cube of bread turns crisp and golden in 1 minute. Meanwhile, dip the chicken pieces in milk. Mix the flour with the baking powder (I use a plastic bag), adding a good seasoning of salt and freshly milled black pepper. Jump the chicken joints up and down in the flour to coat them evenly. Now deep fry them in the oil for 15 minutes, turning them over occasionally. When the chicken joints are cooked, drain them on crumpled greaseproof paper and serve immediately, sprinkled with a little crushed rock salt.

In America Southern Fried Chicken has a traditional accompaniment of fried bananas and corn fritters. I think it's equally nice with some sauté potatoes and a crisp salad.

Spiced Chicken Pilau

(Serves 4)

Not all Indian dishes are as long and as complicated as one would imagine: this one, for instance, can be made very easily at home.

A 2½–3-lb roasting chicken, cut into 8 joints (plus chicken giblets)
2 medium onions, peeled and finely chopped
2 tablespoons groundnut oil
1 heaped teaspoon ground ginger
1 level teaspoon ground turmeric
1 level teaspoon Madras curry powder
¼ pint natural yoghurt
2 cloves garlic, crushed
2 bayleaves, crumbled
1 inch cinnamon stick
1 green pepper, de-seeded and finely chopped
1 cup long-grain rice
2½ cups chicken stock (made with the giblets)
2 cloves
Salt and freshly milled black pepper

Wipe the chicken joints and season them with salt and pepper. Heat the oil in a large saucepan or flameproof casserole and fry the seasoned chicken joints until well browned. Then, using a draining spoon, remove them to a plate and gently fry the chopped onions, pepper and garlic in the fat remaining in the pan. As soon as they're softened (about 6 minutes), stir in the spices, then return the chicken joints to the pan and stir in the yoghurt. Cover the pan and cook gently for about 15 minutes, giving it a shake from time to time. Now uncover the pan and stir in the rice, followed by the stock, bayleaf and cloves. Then bring to simmering point, cover and cook gently for about 20 minutes. After that remove the pan from the heat and leave (covered) until the rice has absorbed the excess liquid. Now taste and season, if it needs it, and serve with some mango chutney.

Mustard Coated Chicken   (Serves 4)

It's best to prepare this 3–4 hours in advance so that the
mustard flavours can penetrate the chicken.

8 small chicken joints (wings and thighs) or a whole chicken
   cut in 8
2 tablespoons English made mustard
1 tablespoon Dijon mustard
2 eggs
5 oz dry white breadcrumbs
Flour
Salt and freshly milled black pepper
Cooking oil

Begin by removing the skins from the chicken joints, then in a
small basin blend together smoothly both the mustards and
the eggs. Now take 2 squares of greaseproof paper: on one
place the breadcrumbs and on the other some flour. Season
each chicken joint with freshly milled black pepper and salt,
and dust with flour. Then dip each one into the mustard
mixture (making sure it's evenly coated) and roll it in the breadcrumbs, patting the crumbs on firmly. Place all the joints on a
large plate and chill for 3 or 4 hours. To cook the chicken
you'll need either a very large frying pan or two smaller ones
with about 1 inch of oil, heated to the stage where a small cube
of bread froths on contact. Fry the chicken joints over a
medium heat for about 20 minutes in all, turning them over
occasionally—they should be crisp and golden. Drain on
crumpled greaseproof paper and serve hot.

Spiced Chicken with Lentils (Serves 6)

For this recipe try to buy the whole brown or green lentils, and don't worry if you haven't got all the relevant spices, you can use curry powder instead—about 2 teaspoons of the hot Madras kind.

A 3½-lb chicken, cut into 6 portions
¾ pint chicken stock made with the giblets
2 medium onions, peeled and sliced
1 clove garlic, crushed
1 heaped teaspoon ground coriander
1 level teaspoon ground ginger
1 teaspoon powdered cumin seed
1 level teaspoon ground turmeric
½–¾ teaspoon chilli powder (depending on how hot you like it)
½ lb whole lentils, soaked in cold water for half an hour
1 tablespoon tomato purée
2 tablespoons groundnut oil
Salt

Pre-heat the oven to mark 4/350 °F

Start by heating the oil in a flameproof casserole and fry the chicken portions to a nice golden colour on all sides. Then set them on one side and add the onions and garlic to the pan. Soften them for about 5 minutes, then stir in the spices and cook for another 5 minutes. Now return the chicken pieces to the casserole and spoon the spicy onion and oil mixture over them. Next add the drained lentils, then mix the tomato purée with the hot chicken stock and pour that in. Now add a little salt and bring everything up to simmering point—and make sure all the lentils are pushed down so that they are almost covered by the liquid. Put a lid on and transfer the casserole to the oven, where it will take about 45 minutes to an hour to cook. Serve with rice and mango chutney.

Harvest Rabbit

(Serves 4)

If you live in the country, then you'll probably know that wild rabbits are very often available at harvest time. However, if you're not lucky enough to get a wild one, a commercially-reared one will do.

1 young rabbit, jointed
4 large carrots, scraped and cut into chunks
4 small onions, peeled and left whole
1 bayleaf
A sprig of thyme
A few parsley stalks
1 pint hot water (see below)
1 tablespoon chopped fresh parsley
Salt and freshly milled black pepper
1 tablespoon butter worked to a paste with 1 tablespoon flour

For the suet-crust pastry:
6 oz self-raising flour
3 oz shredded suet
1 teaspoon grated onion
1 tablespoon chopped fresh parsley
Seasoning

Pre-heat the oven to mark 4/350 °F

Wash the rabbit joints first and place them in a 9½-inch diameter casserole, season with pepper and salt, then scatter in the herbs and tuck the carrots and onions in amongst them. Now pour in the hot water, put a lid on and bake for 30 minutes; then remove the lid and bake for a further 30 minutes, or until the rabbit is tender. Remove the rabbit from the oven and increase the heat to mark 7/425 °F. Add the flour and butter paste, cut into peanut-sized pieces, plus 1 tablespoon of parsley, and stir it in where possible. Now make up a suet-crust pastry with the flour, suet, grated onion and 1 tablespoon of parsley, seasoning with pepper and salt. Add enough cold water to make an elastic dough that leaves the bowl clean, then roll it out to fit inside the casserole, covering the rabbit, etc. Now return the casserole to the oven for 25–35 minutes, or until the suet-crust is browned and puffy. Serve very hot with a green vegetable to go with it.

Note: You can improve this, if you have the time, by boiling the head and ribs to make 1 pint of stock to use instead of water, or use ½ pint of dry cider and ½ pint of water.

Rabbit in Cider   (Serves 4)

As in the previous recipe, if you can get hold of a wild rabbit for this, so much the better.

2 lb rabbit joints (or a medium rabbit jointed)
1 tablespoon oil
1 oz butter
½ lb unsmoked streaky bacon, bought if possible in one piece
    and then cut in cubes
2 medium onions, peeled and chopped
½ pint dry cider
1 heaped tablespoon flour
½ pint stock
½ lb dark-gilled mushrooms, sliced
1 clove garlic, crushed
6 juniper berries, crushed
A sprig of thyme (or ½ teaspoon dried)
Salt and freshly milled black pepper

Begin by heating the butter and oil in a flameproof casserole and frying the rabbit joints quickly to brown them all over. Now remove them to one side and fry the onions, garlic and bacon for about 10 minutes. Then sprinkle in the flour, stir and cook for a minute or two before gradually stirring in the cider and the stock. At this stage add the rabbit joints, together with the thyme and crushed juniper berries. Bring everything to simmering point, then add the sliced mushrooms and a seasoning of salt and freshly milled pepper. Cover and simmer the rabbit very gently for about an hour, or until it's tender.

Roasted Rabbit with Onions and Bacon
(Serves 4)

1 largish rabbit (ask the butcher to joint it for you)
2 large onions, peeled and chopped
½ lb fat streaky bacon
1½ tablespoons seasoned flour
2 oz dripping or butter
Salt and freshly milled black pepper

Pre-heat the oven to mark 4/350 °F

Dust the rabbit joints with seasoned flour and wrap each joint in one or two rashers of streaky bacon. Now arrange them in a roasting tin and season with freshly milled black pepper and just a little salt (because there's some in the bacon). Tuck the pieces of onion in and around the rabbit (putting some pieces underneath the joints), then dot some little knobs of dripping or butter here and there, using about 2 oz in all. Place the roasting tin in the oven and cook for 1 hour, basting with the fat and juices at least 3 times. When it's ready, remove everything to a serving dish, spoon off the fat from the roasting tin and make a gravy to go with it.

FOREQUARTER FRONT

The figures are well-known: it takes 10 lb of grain to get 1 lb of beef. About 40–50 per cent of our beef is grain-fed, therefore each time there is a bad harvest world grain prices rocket (and so does beef). You don't have to be a monetary expert to see that it's a very wasteful way of intensively producing protein.

I don't think we should do without beef altogether, but as the world population increases—and grain shortages along with it—it would be unrealistic to think of the future of meat as anything but doubtful. TVP (see p. 182) has now arrived and laboratory nutritionists are already investigating such phenomena as 'bacterial' proteins. As for us, well perhaps the affluent era of everyday steaks, chops and grills *is* on the way out, but by world standards we still have a lot of meat in this country. However, because it's going to cost us more and more, I feel that from now on we have to make the best possible use of it.

There's no such thing as cheap cuts any more, but forequarter meat (on me that's from the waist up) *is* less expensive and *does* get overlooked, since it needs more careful and longer cooking. Yet if you're prepared to take the trouble, forequarter meat very often has a far better flavour.

I promise that if you were to make a direct comparison you would find that shoulder of lamb has a sweeter flavour than leg: similarly, belly and shoulder of pork compared with leg. And silverside or topside are mere shadows of chuck when it comes to pot-roasting or braising. Flavour is not a feature of intensively reared meat at the best of times, so let us nurture what little we have (lamb being the one exception, of course—the only reliable species of 'free-range' meat left to us). So forward forequarters! as in the following recipes, which may take a little longer to cook but won't be difficult to prepare.

Braised Pork with Prunes   (Serves 4)

1½ lb lean belly of pork or spare ribs, cut into cubes
1 large cooking apple, peeled, cored and sliced
½ lb onions, peeled and sliced
1 clove garlic, crushed
4 oz prunes, halved and stoned
6 juniper berries, crushed
1½ lb potatoes, peeled and thickly sliced
¼ pint dry cider
Lard
A little caster sugar
Butter
½ teaspoon chopped thyme
Salt and freshly milled black pepper

Pre-heat the oven to mark 3/325 °F

Fry the pork in a little lard to brown it nicely, then arrange it
in the bottom of a shallow (and fairly wide) fireproof casserole
or pie dish. Season with pepper and salt and sprinkle over the
crushed juniper berries and the chopped thyme. Now fry the
onion and garlic a little bit, and put it round the pork with a
few pieces of prune tucked here and there. Next arrange the
apple slices all over and give them a very slight dusting of
caster sugar. Finally, arrange the thick potato slices on top,
making them overlap one another. Season with some more
pepper and salt, dot with a few flecks of butter and pour in the
cider. Cover and bake for 1½ hours. When the cooking time's
up, raise the heat to mark 8/450 °F, remove the lid and cook
for a further 20 minutes or so—or until the potatoes have
turned a lovely golden brown (or brown them under a hot
grill).

Roast Lamb with Coriander (Serves 3)

In the winter, when only imported lamb is reasonably priced, this is a good way to jazz up half a shoulder.

½ shoulder of lamb
1 clove garlic, cut into slivers
1 tablespoon coriander seeds
Dripping
Stock or dry cider

Pre-heat the oven to mark 5/375 °F

Place the meat in a roasting tin and, using a small sharp knife, make about 6–8 evenly placed incisions in it. Into these slits push slivers of garlic and about a tablespoon of coriander seeds (crushed a bit first, using either a pestle and mortar or the back of a tablespoon). Add a knob of dripping to the roasting tin and roast for 30 minutes to the pound, basting with the juices from time to time. When the lamb is cooked, carve it into thick slices and keep warm. Then strain off the fat from the roasting tin and add a little stock or dry cider to the juices to make a gravy. Redcurrant jelly is a nice accompaniment.

Beef in Cider

(Serves 6)

This is an inexpensive dish, although special enough for a dinner party—quite simply a classic boeuf bourguignonne only made with cider and every bit as good.

2 lb chuck steak, cut into largish chunks
½ lb streaky bacon in one piece (smoked or green)
¾ lb small onions, peeled and left whole
1 medium onion, peeled and sliced
2 cloves garlic, chopped
2 sprigs fresh thyme (or ½ teaspoon dried)
1 bayleaf
1 rounded tablespoon plain flour
¾ pint dry cider
¼ lb dark flat mushrooms, sliced
Beef dripping
Salt and freshly milled black pepper

Pre-heat the oven to mark 2/300 °F

Start off by melting some beef dripping in a very large solid frying pan and frying the sliced onion for 5 minutes. Then turn the heat right up, add the cubes of meat and brown them quickly on all sides, tossing them around frequently. Next sprinkle in the flour, stir it around to soak up all the juices, then gradually pour in the cider—stirring all the time—and add the chopped garlic and herbs. Season with salt and pepper, then pour the whole lot into a casserole, put a lid on and cook in the oven for 2 hours. Now, using a bit more beef dripping, fry the small onions and bacon to colour them lightly, and add them to the casserole together with the sliced mushrooms. Then put the lid back on and cook for a further hour. This is nice served with buttered noodles or onion-flavoured rice.

87

Pork and Kidney Hotpot   (Serves 3–4)

I love to use juniper berries with pork dishes, but if you haven't got—or can't get—any, just leave them out.

1 lb lean belly of pork, cut into cubes
1 pork kidney, trimmed and sliced
1 medium cooking apple, peeled and thinly sliced
1 largish onion, peeled and chopped
2 tablespoons well-seasoned flour
½ teaspoon dried sage
1 clove garlic, crushed
2 lb potatoes, peeled and thickly sliced
½ pint stock or dry cider
Lard
Butter
Salt and freshly milled black pepper

Pre-heat the oven to mark 5/375 °F

Melt some lard in a largish frying pan, then dust the pieces of pork in seasoned flour and fry them to a nice golden brown all round. Now, using a draining spoon, transfer them to a pie dish (I use an old pie dish of about 2½ pints capacity). Next fry the slices of kidney (which should also have been dipped in seasoned flour) and tuck those in amongst the pork; then sprinkle the sage over the pork, followed by some salt and pepper. Now soften the onion and garlic in the frying pan for about 10 minutes, then sprinkle them over the meat, followed by the slices of apple. Next pour in the stock or cider and finally top everything with the slices of potato overlapping each other. Season the potatoes, brush them with a little melted butter and bake the hotpot in the oven for approximately 1 hour, or until the potatoes are a golden brown and the pork is tender.

Baked Stuffed Breast of Lamb (Serves 2)

For this ask your butcher for a nice large breast of lamb and
have him remove the bones for you.

1 large breast of lamb, boned

For the stuffing:
2 oz fresh breadcrumbs
Grated rind of ½ lemon
¼ whole nutmeg, grated
1 tablespoon chopped fresh mint
1 tablespoon chopped fresh parsley
1 medium onion, peeled and very finely chopped
1 teaspoon finely crushed rosemary
1 small egg, beaten
Salt and freshly milled black pepper

Pre-heat the oven to mark 4/350 °F

In a mixing bowl, mix the breadcrumbs and onion, parsley,
mint and rosemary, then add the nutmeg and lemon rind.
Mix thoroughly and add a good seasoning of pepper and salt.
Now stir in the beaten egg to bind the stuffing together, then
spread the stuffing evenly over the breast of lamb and roll the
lamb up gently and not too tightly. Tuck the flap end over
and tie the meat in 3 places with string—again not too tightly.
Press back any bits of stuffing that fall out, wrap the meat in
foil, place it on a roasting tin and bake for 1½ hours. Then unwrap the foil, baste with the juices and brown for a further ½
hour, basting again once or twice. Serve the meat cut in thick
slices with thin gravy made with the juices, and some redcurrant jelly.

Pork Rissoles with Spiced Apple Sauce

(Serves 4)

These are lovely served with creamy mashed potatoes and cooked dried peas.

1 lb shoulder of pork, cut into chunks
1 onion, peeled and quartered
4 oz breadcrumbs (white or brown)
½ teaspoon dried sage
¼ teaspoon ground mace
1 teaspoon salt
Freshly milled black pepper
1 cooking apple, peeled, cored and quartered
A little butter

For the sauce:
1 oz butter
½ lb cooking apples, peeled and chopped
½ small onion, peeled and chopped
1 tablespoon water
Freshly grated nutmeg
A couple of pinches ground cloves
Sugar to taste

Pre-heat the oven to mark 5/375°F

Pass the pork, onion, bread and apple through a mincer and mix them thoroughly with the remaining rissole ingredients. Form the mixture into balls and arrange in the base of a small buttered roasting tin. Cover with some buttered foil and bake in the top half of the oven for 45 minutes. Then remove the foil, raise the oven temperature to mark 6/400°F and continue to bake for a further 30 minutes, basting now and then, until the rissoles are nicely browned on top. Meanwhile, to make the sauce, soften the onion in 1 oz of butter for 10 minutes, then stir in the sliced apple and 1 tablespoon of water. Put a lid on and simmer till soft, then add a little freshly grated nutmeg, a couple of pinches of ground cloves and enough sugar to taste. Beat the sauce till fluffy, and serve hot with the rissoles.

Stuffed Shoulder of Lamb with Rice and Olives

(Serves 4)

3–5 lb shoulder of lamb (ask the butcher to bone it for you
   and give you the trimmings)
2 oz chopped onion
3 oz rice, cooked (that's 3 oz dry weight before cooking)
3–4 oz minced lamb, from the trimmings
12 Spanish stuffed olives (6 of them quartered or sliced for
   the stuffing)
1 egg
1 clove garlic, crushed
Chopped parsley
¼ teaspoon finely crushed rosemary
Salt and freshly milled pepper

For the gravy:
¾ oz flour
½ pint stock

Pre-heat the oven to mark 6/400 °F

Begin by seasoning the inside surfaces of the meat with the
crushed rosemary, salt and pepper. Then mix the minced
lamb with some crushed garlic, the cooked rice, chopped onion,
chopped olives, parsley and a little beaten egg. Spread the
stuffing over the meat, then roll the meat up as neatly as possible into a cylindrical shape. Now tie loops of string round it
at 2-inch intervals, and season the surface with salt and pepper.
Next place the meat in a roasting tin and roast the joint for 25
minutes to the pound. When it's cooked, remove the string and
place it on a warmed serving dish to keep it warm whilst you
make up the gravy. Using the juices in the pan, stir in the
flour, then add the stock bit by bit, followed by the whole
olives. Serve the meat with the gravy separate—and some new
carrots and new potatoes would be a nice accompaniment.

Pot Roast of Pork with Cabbage and Juniper

(Serves 6–8)

An obliging butcher will bone and roll a shoulder joint for you for this.

3 lb shoulder of pork, boned and rolled
1¼ lb white cabbage, sliced
3 tablespoons pork dripping (or lard)
2 medium onions, peeled and sliced
1 clove garlic, sliced
2 carrots, scraped and sliced
¼ teaspoon dried thyme—or a sprig of fresh
12 juniper berries, crushed
A little chopped parsley
Salt and freshly milled black pepper

Pre-heat the oven to mark 3/325 °F

Wipe the joint as dry as possible, then melt the dripping in an extra large flameproof casserole and, with the heat fairly high, brown the pork steadily all over. Then remove it to a plate while you fry the sliced onions, garlic and carrots for about 10 minutes or so. Now replace the joint in the casserole and bring it up to sizzling point. Sprinkle it with salt, pepper, the dried thyme and the juniper berries, then put a lid on and transfer it to the oven to bake for 1 hour, giving it a basting with the juices about halfway through the cooking time. Meanwhile slice the cabbage. Bring a large saucepan of salted water to the boil, add the sliced cabbage, bring back to the boil to cook for 3 minutes, then rinse in cold water and drain in a colander, pressing out any excess liquid. When the hour is up, remove the casserole from the oven, add the drained cabbage and stir it into the juices in the casserole. Now re-heat until bubbling, cover again and replace in the oven for a further hour (once more basting the joint midway). When the time's up, remove the joint and slice into serving pieces, and taste and season the cabbage mixture. Arrange the sliced pork over the cabbage, sprinkle with chopped parsley and serve with some crunchy roast potatoes.

92

Pork with Summer Vegetables   (Serves 2)

Because lamb is so popular during the summer months, pork is very often down in price. (Let's hope!)

2 spare rib chops
4 small or 2 large new carrots, scraped and sliced
6 shallots or small onions, peeled and left whole
¾ lb fresh peas (weighed in the pods)
1 dessertspoon lard
½ teaspoon chopped rosemary (fresh if possible)
¼ pint boiling water
Salt and freshly milled black pepper

Pre-heat the oven to mark 3/325 °F

First heat the lard in a frying pan and brown the chops, colouring them a nice golden brown on both sides. Then transfer them to a large ovenproof dish (I use a 3-pint oval pie dish) and sprinkle them with the rosemary. Now add the whole shallots and the sliced carrots to the pan, and cook to colour them a little too. Then, using a draining spoon, arrange them round the pork, season and pour in ¼ pint of boiling water. Cover the dish with a double sheet of foil (or a lid) and transfer to the oven for an hour. Meanwhile shell the peas. When the hour is up, stir the peas down into the juices, taste and add a little more seasoning, if necessary; then re-cover with the foil and cook for an extra 20–30 minutes, depending on the age of the peas. Serve with new potatoes tossed in butter and snipped chives.

Note: If you can't get any small onions, use a couple of ordinary sized, sliced.

Mutton Pot Pie

The bones in the meat give this a delicious sauce, whilst the suet crust on top makes it very filling and substantial—in fact, don't plan to do anything much for a while after eating it.

8 large pieces middle neck of lamb
2 medium onions, peeled and chopped
3 medium carrots, scraped and sliced
1 lb potatoes, peeled and sliced
2 tablespoons pearl barley
1 teaspoon dried thyme
1 clove garlic, crushed
2 tablespoons seasoned flour
Salt and freshly milled black pepper

For the suet-crust pastry:
8 oz self-raising flour
4 oz shredded suet
Salt and freshly milled black pepper

Pre-heat the oven to mark 2/300 °F

Trim any excess fat from the lamb, then dust the pieces with seasoned flour and arrange a layer of meat in the bottom of a heavy flameproof casserole, about 4 pints capacity, followed by a sprinkling of the crushed garlic and herbs, then a layer of vegetables and a tablespoon of pearl barley. Season well. Repeat the layers and finally add enough boiling water to almost cover everything. Then put on the lid and cook in the oven for about 2 hours. Just before the end of the cooking time, make the pastry by mixing the flour and suet with some pepper, salt and just enough cold water to make a smooth, elastic dough. Now remove the casserole and turn the heat right up to mark 7/425 °F. Roll the pastry out to a round big enough to just fit inside the rim of the casserole. Put it on and make a small hole in the centre. Return the casserole to the oven (without a lid this time) and let the pastry cook for 30 minutes. Serve immediately.

Brown Beef Stew with Dumplings

1 lb of chuck steak will serve 4 easily in this recipe, which includes plenty of vegetables *and* some fluffy dumplings.

1 lb chuck steak, cubed
2 oz beef dripping
4 smallish onions, peeled and left whole
1 medium turnip, peeled and cut into chunks
½ swede, peeled and cut into chunks
6 small carrots, scraped and left whole
1½ tablespoons plain flour
1 bayleaf
½ teaspoon dried mixed herbs
1½ teaspoons Worcestershire sauce
1 pint boiling water
A knob of butter
Salt and freshly milled black pepper

For the dumplings:
4 oz self-raising flour
2 oz shredded suet
1 tablespoon fresh chopped parsley
Salt and freshly milled black pepper

Pre-heat the oven to mark 2/300 °F

For this you'll need a flameproof 4½–5-pint casserole and a large frying pan. First of all you heat the dripping till smoking hot and brown the pieces of meat in it quickly, tossing them around—they should be a deep brown, nutty colour. Now take a draining spoon and transfer them to the casserole. Then, lowering the heat a little, start to fry the prepared vegetables. These, too, should be browned and caramelised a bit at the edges (this is very important for the flavour of the stew). As they brown, transfer them to the casserole to join the meat. Now to the juices left in the frying pan add a knob of butter, allow it to melt, then stir in the flour and, with the heat reasonably high, keep stirring and let the flour get brown before gradually adding the hot water, still stirring, as you would for white sauce. When you've added all the water, pour the gravy into the casserole over the meat and vegetables, add some salt and pepper, the bayleaf, herbs and Worcestershire sauce, put a tight lid on and transfer it to the oven to cook for 3 hours.

Just before the end of the cooking time, sift the flour into a basin, mix in the suet, parsley, pepper and salt, and enough cold water to make a smooth elastic dough that leaves the bowl clean. Then divide the dough and roll it into 10 or 12 small balls. Now transfer the casserole to the top of the stove, give it a gentle heat to keep it just simmering, then pop the dumplings in all over the top (don't push them into the liquid, just sit them on top). Put the lid back on, and let the stew simmer for 25 minutes. Then serve immediately—one snag with dumplings is that they don't like hanging around.

Porc au Choux
(Serves 3–4)

Try to get lean belly of pork cut from the thick end; alternatively, you could use cubed spare rib chops.

1¼ lb belly of pork, cubed
4 oz streaky bacon, rinded and cut into small cubes
1 large onion, peeled and chopped
1 clove garlic, crushed
2 tablespoons oil
10 juniper berries, crushed
½ pint dry cider
1 lb white cabbage, shredded
Chopped fresh parsley
Salt and freshly milled black pepper

Pre-heat the oven to mark 3/325 °F

Heat the oil in a flameproof casserole and soften the onion and garlic in it for about 5 minutes. Then add the cubes of bacon and pork and, with the heat fairly high, brown them to a golden colour, tossing them frequently around. Now lower the heat, add the shredded cabbage and stir to get it all nicely coated with oil; then add the crushed juniper berries followed by the cider. Season with salt and pepper, then put a tight-fitting lid on and cook in the oven for about 1–1¼ hours.

Although this tastes very good, its appearance is deceptive and needs a sprinkling of chopped parsley to 'jazz' it up a bit.

Steak and Onions in Guinness (Serves 2)

If you long for a thick, juicy, grilled steak and can't afford it, try this recipe with braising steak—it's every bit as good.

¾–1 lb lean braising steak (in 2 pieces)
2 large onions, peeled and cut into rings
¼ pint Guinness
Beef dripping
Salt and freshly milled black pepper

Pre-heat the oven to mark 2/300 °F

In a frying pan melt the dripping and fry the onion rings over a medium heat until they're nicely tinged with brown and starting to caramelise all round the edges. Now remove them to a plate, add a little more dripping to the pan if you need to and brown the meat over a fairly high heat. This browning (on both sides) will help the flavour. Next take a shallow gratin dish or casserole, arrange a layer of onion in it, place the steak on top and season well. Add another layer of onion, pour in the stout, cover closely with either a lid or a double sheet of foil and cook near the top of the oven for 2½–3 hours, or until the steak is tender. This goes very well with some creamed potatoes —and with the oven on for that length of time, you might contemplate cooking another casserole at the same time.

Devilled Pork Slices

(Serves 3)

For this ask the butcher for 6 lean slices of pork cut from the thick end of the belly.

6 lean slices belly of pork (about 1¼ lb)

For the sauce:
1 tablespoon tomato purée
1 tablespoon water
1 tablespoon Worcestershire sauce
1 tablespoon wine vinegar
1 teaspoon clear honey
1 teaspoon English made mustard
1 clove garlic, crushed
1 level dessertspoon ground ginger
Salt and freshly milled black pepper

Pre-heat the oven to mark 6/400 °F

Trim the rind and any excess fat from the pork, arrange the slices in a single layer in a roasting tin and season them a little. Then thoroughly combine all the sauce ingredients together in a basin and pour this mixture over the pork. Cover the tin with foil and bake in the oven for about 40 minutes. After that, remove the foil and bake for a further 20 minutes or so. Now arrange the pork slices on a warmed serving dish. Keep them warm whilst you spoon off any fat from the roasting tin, then add about 4 tablespoons of hot water (potato water would be ideal) and stir over a medium heat, scraping the sides and base of the tin. When it reaches simmering point, pour the gravy over the pork and serve with creamy mashed potato.

Ground Beef Curry

(Serves 3)

This is a good way to 'uplift' 1 lb of mince, but it *has* to be good-quality mince from a reliable supplier.

1 lb good-quality minced beef
¾ lb onions, peeled and sliced
1 small apple, finely chopped
2 tablespoons groundnut oil
2 cloves garlic, crushed
1 dessertspoon Madras curry powder (or more or less,
   depending on how hot you like it)
½ teaspoon ground ginger
½ teaspoon ground turmeric
¼ pint natural yoghurt
¼ pint hot water mixed with 1 heaped teaspoon tomato purée
Salt and freshly milled black pepper

Pre-heat the oven to mark 2/300 °F

First of all, in a flameproof casserole, heat the oil and soften the sliced onion in it for about 10 minutes. Then turn up the heat, stir in the minced beef and move it around until it's all nicely browned and separate—a wooden fork is good for this. Now turn the heat down, stir in the spices, garlic and some salt and pepper, followed by the yoghurt and the tomato-and-water mixture. Stir thoroughly, put a lid on and cook in the oven for 2 hours. Serve with rice and mango chutney.

Note: This *could* be cooked on top of the stove if watched carefully.

Fidget Pie

There are many versions of this famous English dish. I don't claim this recipe to be the authentic one, but it's very good.

1½ lb boned gammon forehock
1 lb potatoes, peeled and very thinly sliced
¾ lb onions, peeled, halved and very thinly sliced
¾ lb cooking apples, peeled, cored and sliced
½ pint dry cider or hot water
Freshly milled black pepper (but no salt)

For the pastry:
8 oz plain flour
4 oz lard
A pinch of salt
Water to mix
Milk to glaze

Pre-heat the oven to mark 5/375 °F

First remove the rind and excess fat from the gammon, and cut the meat into quite small pieces. Then gather together all the rest of the ingredients for the pie, take a large 3½-pint pie dish and layer the ingredients in this order: first the gammon, then the onions and apples and finally the potatoes—about 3 layers of each, finishing off with a layer of potatoes. As you go, sprinkle a little freshly milled pepper in between the layers. Now pour in the cider. Next prepare the pastry and roll it out. Line the rim of the pie dish with pastry strips and dampen them before covering with a pastry lid. Now pinch the edges to seal, and decorate the top of the pie (any pastry left over can be re-rolled and cut into pastry 'leaves'). Lastly, brush the pastry with milk, make a steam hole in the centre of the pie and sit the pie dish on a baking sheet. After 30 minutes reduce the heat to mark 3/325 °F and cook for a further hour.

Bacon with Dumplings and Parsley Sauce

This is both filling and comforting on a really cold day.

A piece of bacon collar weighing about 1½ lb
4 smallish onions, peeled and left whole
2 large carrots, scraped and cut in half
1 bayleaf
A few parsley stalks

For the dumplings:
3 oz self-raising flour
1½ oz shredded suet
Seasoning

For the sauce:
1 oz butter
1 oz flour
¼ pint milk
½ pint stock (use the bacon water)
2 heaped tablespoons chopped fresh parsley

Place the bacon in a good *large* casserole (it must be large enough to take all the other things). Then cover with cold water, bring to the boil and throw out the water. This will take care of any saltiness. Now pour on some fresh boiling water to just cover the bacon, add the bayleaf and a few parsley stalks, put a lid on and simmer gently for 30 minutes. Then add the peeled whole onions and halved carrots, replace the lid and continue simmering for a further 20 minutes. Meanwhile make the dumplings by mixing the flour, suet and some seasoning with enough cold water to make a smooth elastic dough, and roll it into 8 small dumplings. When the 20 minutes cooking time is up, ladle out ½ pint of the bacon stock into a measuring jug. Then, keeping the rest simmering, pop the dumplings in around the bacon—don't push them down, let them float—cover and cook for a further 25 minutes. Meanwhile make a parsley sauce with the butter, flour, milk, reserved bacon stock (plus a little extra if you need it) and the chopped parsley. Serve the bacon cut in slices with the onion, dumplings and carrots, and the sauce in a jug.

Navarin of Lamb   (Serves 4)

This is an excellent way of serving middle neck of lamb. I like it best made in the summer with new potatoes, but it can be made in the winter using chunks of old potatoes instead.

2 lb middle neck of lamb, cut into pieces
Dripping
2 tablespoons flour
1¼ pints hot water
1 level tablespoon tomato purée
1 clove garlic, crushed
½ teaspoon dried thyme (or a sprig of fresh thyme)
8 small onions, peeled and left whole
6 baby turnips, peeled and quartered
6 small carrots, scraped and cut into 1-inch lengths
12 very small new potatoes, scraped
1 level teaspoon brown sugar
Salt and freshly milled black pepper

Begin by heating some dripping in a large flameproof casserole. Trim any excess fat from the meat, then season the pieces with salt and pepper, and fry them in the hot fat until brown on all sides. Now sprinkle in the flour and, keeping the heat fairly low, stir it around to soak up the juices. Next add the hot water, tomato purée, crushed garlic and thyme. Then bring everything gently up to simmering point, giving it a stir now and then. Put the lid on and cook very gently for 45 minutes. While that's happening, using a little more dripping fry the prepared onions, turnips and carrots. When the 45 minutes is up, add these vegetables to the casserole along with the scraped potatoes and bring to simmering point again. Add the sugar, cover and continue to simmer gently for a further 45 minutes.

Pork Chops Boulangère   (Serves 4)

For this you can use spare rib chops or belly of pork strips—
allow 1 per person.

4 large potatoes, peeled and thinly sliced
1 large onion, peeled and finely chopped
1 tablespoon seasoned flour
¾ teaspoon dried sage
¼ pint milk
½ pint stock (or water)
1 tablespoon oil
½ oz butter, plus a little extra
Salt and freshly milled black pepper

Pre-heat the oven to mark 4/350 °F

Dust the chops in seasoned flour, heat ½ oz of butter and the oil
in a large frying pan and fry the chops on both sides until
nicely browned. Then remove the pan from the heat. Now
butter a small roasting tin and put a layer of half the potatoes
and onion over the base, seasoning them with salt and pepper.
Lay the browned chops on top and sprinkle them with sage,
salt and pepper. Cover them with the rest of the onions and
then with a final layer of sliced potatoes. Next pour over the
mixed stock and milk, add a few flecks of butter, cover with
greased foil and bake in the oven for about an hour. Then take
off the foil, raise the heat to mark 5/375 °F for a further ½–¾
hour, or until the potatoes are browned on top. This is delicious
served with spiced red cabbage.

Boiled Bacon and Pease Pudding

(Serves 6)

Try to get green split peas for this, but yellow will do if you can't buy the green.

A 2¾-lb piece boned rolled bacon forehock
1 large carrot, scraped and cut in chunks
1 onion, peeled, halved and each half stuck with 2 cloves
1 bayleaf
A few parsley stalks
1 lb green split peas
2 oz butter
¼–½ teaspoon caster sugar
Salt and freshly milled black pepper

Start off by placing the bacon in a large deep pot and covering it with cold water; then bring it to the boil and as soon as the water reaches boiling point, throw it out and start again with a new lot of cold water. Then add the onion, carrot, bayleaf and parsley stalks. Now wash the peas in a sieve and put them in a large section of linen cloth or double gauze (about 17 inches square). Tie it very tightly, but leave the peas plenty of room to expand during the cooking, then pop the bundle of peas into the pot to cook alongside the bacon. Now put a lid on, bring to simmering point, then turn the heat down and simmer gently for about 1¼ hours. After that, have ready a bowl (warmed) containing the butter. Switch off the heat under the pot, remove the bundle of peas, untie it and scrape the peas into the warmed bowl. Now mash them to a purée. Taste and add the sugar, salt and freshly milled pepper, and if you think the mixture is still on the dry side, add a spoonful of the cooking liquor to moisten it while you skin and carve the bacon. Serve the bacon with the pease pudding on the table for everyone to help themselves—and some parsley sauce would make it extra specially good.

Traditional Cornish Pasties

The quantities given here will make 4 large pasties for 4
people; alternatively, smaller ones could be made for taking on
a journey or picnic.

1 lb chuck steak
1 large onion, peeled and chopped very small
1 medium potato, peeled and cut into very thin slices
1 medium turnip, peeled and cut into very thin slices
½ teaspoon mixed herbs
Salt and freshly milled black pepper
1 lb shortcrust pastry (made with 10 oz plain flour, 5 oz lard,
    a pinch each salt and pepper, cold water to mix)
1 egg, beaten

Pre-heat the oven to mark 8/425 °F

Cut the steak up into very small thin pieces and mix it with
the potato, onion, turnip and herbs, seasoning well with salt
and freshly milled black pepper. Then make the pastry,
divide it into 4 and roll each piece out on a lightly floured
surface to a round approximately 8 inches in diameter. Place
a quarter of the meat mixture in the centre of each round of
pastry, then dampen the edges with beaten egg, pull them up
to meet in the centre and seal them very thoroughly. Knock
up the edges and flute them, then brush the pasties all over
with beaten egg, make two small steam holes in each one and
place all 4 of them on a lightly greased baking sheet and bake
in the oven for 15 minutes. Then reduce the heat to mark
4/350 °F and continue cooking them for another 60 minutes.

Steak and Kidney Hotpot (Serves 6)

If you love the delicious combination of steak and kidney but aren't too keen on suet pastry, then this recipe is for you, because instead of pastry it has a crust of thickly sliced potatoes on top.

1½ lb chuck steak, trimmed and cut into bite-sized cubes
½ lb ox kidney, trimmed and cut fairly small
2 lb potatoes, peeled and cut into thick slices
2 medium onions, peeled and roughly chopped
1 rounded tablespoon flour
½ pint beef stock
¾ teaspoon Worcestershire sauce
Beef dripping
Melted butter
Salt and freshly milled black pepper

Pre-heat the oven to mark 2/300 °F

First melt some beef dripping in a large, wide-based saucepan and fry the onion in it to soften for about 5 minutes or so; then turn the heat right up, add the cubes of beef and kidney and cook them to a nutty brown colour—keep stirring and turning the meat as it browns. Now lower the heat a bit, sprinkle in the flour and stir it around to soak up the meat juices. Season well, add the Worcestershire sauce, then gradually stir in the stock and bring to simmering point. Next pour the meat mixture into a casserole or pie dish and arrange the thickly sliced potatoes in layers all over the meat. Season the potatoes, brush them with melted butter, then cover the casserole with a lid or foil and bake in the oven for 2½–3 hours. Before serving remove the lid and brown the potatoes under a very hot grill to get them really crisp.

Beef and Tomato Stew

(Serves 4–6)

This is a good recipe for using up over-ripe tomatoes that are too soft for a salad.

2 lb chuck steak
3 tablespoons oil
2 onions, peeled and chopped
1 lb tomatoes, skinned and thickly sliced
1 fat clove garlic, crushed
1 heaped teaspoon dried basil
½ teaspoon brown sugar
Salt and freshly milled black pepper

Pre-heat the oven to mark 2/300 °F

First trim the meat, then cut it into 1–1½-inch cubes. Then heat the oil in a flameproof casserole and fry the meat over a fairly high heat until the cubes are nicely browned. Now add the chopped onions and garlic to the pan, turn the heat down a bit and continue to cook for a further 10 minutes, or until the onions are softened. Next add the tomatoes to the casserole with the basil and some salt and freshly milled black pepper. Stir well, cover the casserole and transfer to the oven to cook slowly for about 2–2½ hours, or until the meat is tender. Then taste and sprinkle in the sugar, and additional salt and freshly milled black pepper if it needs it. This is delicious served with buttered noodles.

Baked Stuffed Cabbage Leaves   (Serves 4–5)

This is an anglicised version of the Greek dolmades—stuffed vine leaves.

A 2–3-lb head of green cabbage
1 tablespoon oil
1 tablespoon butter
1 onion, peeled and finely chopped
1 clove garlic, crushed
1 lb lean minced chuck steak
2 oz cooked rice (that's 2 oz raw weight)
1 tablespoon tomato purée
1 tablespoon chopped parsley
½ teaspoon dried marjoram
½ teaspoon ground cinnamon
Salt and freshly milled black pepper
A 14-oz can Italian tomatoes

Pre-heat the oven to mark 3/325 °F

First bring a large saucepan of salted water to the boil and place the cabbage in the water, stalk end up. Next bring the water back to the boil and simmer for about 8 minutes; then remove the cabbage and leave it to cool. Working with the cabbage still stalk end up, take a sharp knife and cut the large outer leaves from the main stalk and peel them off one by one. Drain the leaves on kitchen paper—you'll need about 15 leaves altogether. The centre can be used for something else. Now heat the oil and butter together and fry the chopped onion with the garlic gently until the onion is soft and golden. Then add the minced beef and brown it, turning the heat up a bit. Then mix in the rice, parsley, cinnamon, marjoram and tomato purée, seasoning well. Remove the pan and let the mixture cool. Now make a V-shaped cut to remove the thickest part of the stalk from the base of each leaf, place about a tablespoon of stuffing in the centre of each leaf, fold in the sides and roll the leaf up tightly. Then pack the rolled leaves closely together in a casserole and pour the can of tomatoes over; cover and cook in the oven for 1½–2 hours.

Oxtail Soup

Tripe and Onions

Liver and Kidney

OFFAL
BUT I LIKE YOU!

Really 'like' isn't quite the word. Offal is either loved or hated (how many luke-warm offal eaters do you know?). But I must be careful here: often it's indelicate promotion that is to blame. We've all seen those ghastly technicolour pictures in magazines that thrust the whole lot at us in its raw state. Ugh!

The word itself is scarcely a euphemism (Margaret Costa in her delightful *Four Seasons Cookbook* calls it, pointedly, 'Awful Offal'). I frequently call it 'Spare Parts', because that's what it is—lots of nutritious bits and pieces full of potential and flavour. In Britain we've never really made the most of it because we've always had so much meat anyway. But now the time has come to learn from our French cousins, who have always had to make every bit of precious meat go as far as possible.

Fear not, I'm not about to offer you a Pig's Tail Ragout or some baked stuffed intestines. Instead I'm sticking to the more familiar and available liver and kidneys etc. which, although they are expensive, seem to go much further (so you need much less to make a meal). Once again, though, I do stress the seasons: English lamb's liver and kidney will be plentiful from June to October. From January to May imported lamb from places like New Zealand will be the best bet. Oxtails, ox kidney and liver will all be at their cheapest in the winter from about October; pork offal seems to be plentiful all the year round.

Braised Stuffed Hearts

(Serves 4–6)

6 lambs' hearts

For the stuffing:
3 tablespoons butter
1 small onion, peeled and finely chopped
2 oz fresh white breadcrumbs
1 small cooking apple, peeled and chopped
Rind and juice of 1 orange
¼ teaspoon dried thyme
¼ teaspoon dried marjoram
3 tablespoons chopped parsley
Salt and freshly milled black pepper

Then you need:
Seasoned flour
1 tablespoon butter
1 tablespoon oil
1 large onion, peeled and chopped
¼ pint dry cider
¼ pint stock or water
2 teaspoons each butter and flour worked to a paste
1 teaspoon redcurrant jelly

Pre-heat the oven to mark 4/350 °F

First wash the hearts thoroughly, and with a pair of scissors cut out all the tubes and the dividing wall in the centre of each heart (this is to make a neat pocket for the stuffing). Now prepare the stuffing by first heating the butter in a small saucepan and gently frying the onion until softened. Mix the onion and any fat in the pan with the remaining stuffing ingredients and season with salt and pepper. Now stuff the cavities in the hearts with the mixture and secure them at the top with small skewers. Roll the hearts in seasoned flour next, then brown in a casserole in the remaining butter and the oil. Stir in the chopped onion, cook this over a gentle heat until softened, then add the stock and cider. Bring to simmering point, cover and cook in the oven for about 2½–3 hours, or until the hearts are tender. When cooked, drain and arrange the hearts in a warmed serving dish. Bring the remaining pan juices to the boil and add small pieces of the butter and flour paste, stirring quickly. Then add the redcurrant jelly, taste and season. Pour the sauce over the hearts and serve.

Pork Kidneys with Mustard Cream Sauce   (Serves 4)

Pork kidneys soaked overnight have a much milder flavour and, as they're fairly reasonably priced, it's worth going to the trouble.

4 pork kidneys, soaked overnight in cold water
1 large onion, peeled and chopped
1 clove garlic, crushed
2 oz lard
¼ pint stock or hot water
¼ pint dry cider
1½ teaspoons English mustard powder
1½ teaspoons genuine French mustard (Dijon)
A generous pinch thyme
2 tablespoons cream
1 teaspoon plain flour
A pinch cayenne pepper
Salt and freshly milled black pepper

First put the kettle on to boil, then after soaking the kidneys, slice them across into ¼-inch thick medallion-shaped slices and snip out the white cores using a pair of scissors. Now transfer them to a sieve and rinse them with a kettleful of boiling water; leave them to drain thoroughly and dry them in some kitchen paper. Next, in a cooking pot, melt the lard and soften the onion and garlic in it for 5 minutes. Then turn the heat up to high, add the drained and dried kidneys and brown them on all sides. Next lower the heat and stir in the flour to soak up the juices before adding the stock, cider, thyme and seasoning. Now put a lid on and simmer gently for 45 minutes. Meanwhile mix the mustards with the cream, add a pinch of cayenne pepper, then stir this into the cooked kidneys. Cook for a minute or two, then serve with buttered noodles (see p. 160), or rice.

Spiced Kidneys in Yoghurt   (Serves 2)

The imported frozen lambs' kidneys we get in the winter are never quite good enough to be served 'straight' but are perfectly good in a curry like this.

6 lambs' kidneys, skinned
2 medium-sized onions, peeled and thinly sliced
1 clove garlic, crushed
2 tablespoons groundnut oil
1 tablespoon tomato purée
2 teaspoons powdered coriander
1 teaspoon turmeric
¼ teaspoon cumin seeds
¼ pint yoghurt
¼ pint stock
Salt
About ¼ teaspoon chilli powder, or according to how hot you like it

To prepare the kidneys, halve them lengthways and snip out the cores using a sharp pair of kitchen scissors. Now heat the oil in a saucepan and fry the kidneys over a fairly high heat until lightly browned; then transfer them to a plate using a draining spoon. Next fry the sliced onion and garlic in the juices remaining in the pan until the onions are softened and golden. Then stir in the tomato purée, spices and yoghurt, and add the stock. Bring the sauce to simmering point, and continue to simmer very gently for about 15 minutes. Now taste it and flavour the sauce with salt and as much chilli powder as you want—but be careful, it is lethal if you add too much. Then return the kidneys (and any juices) to the pan, cover and simmer gently for 20 minutes. Taste again and season if it needs it. This is nice served with buttered noodles, and an extra dollop of yoghurt if available.

Kidney Stroganoff

(Serves 4)

I think a Stroganoff made with lambs' kidneys is even nicer than one made with fillet steak.

12 lambs' kidneys
1 medium onion
½ lb mushrooms
A 5-oz carton soured cream
2½ oz butter
Freshly grated nutmeg
Salt and freshly milled black pepper

Begin by peeling the onion and slicing it into very thin rings. Now slice the rings in half and separate them to give you moon-shaped slivers. Melt 2 oz of the butter in a large frying pan and gently soften the onion in it for 10 minutes. Meanwhile wipe the mushrooms, slice the stalks and caps thinly, then add them to the onion, stirring them around, and cook for a further 5 minutes. The kidneys should be first skinned and the cores snipped out and then cut into the thinnest slices possible. Turn the heat up a bit under the pan, add the kidney slices and brown them quickly, constantly turning the pieces over. Now turn the heat right down and stir in the soured cream, season with salt, pepper and nutmeg, and let everything simmer very gently for 5 minutes. Just before serving, stir in ½ oz of butter, then serve immediately with plain boiled rice.

Liver and Bacon Kebabs with Stuffing

(Serves 4)

I like to serve these with brown rice and a homemade tomato sauce.

¾ lb lambs' liver
About 6 rashers streaky bacon, rinded and cut in small squares

For the stuffing:
4 oz fresh white breadcrumbs
2 oz dripping or butter, melted
1 teaspoon grated onion
½ teaspoon mixed herbs
A pinch powdered mace
1 egg
About 2 tablespoons milk (to bind)
Salt and freshly milled black pepper
1½ oz extra melted dripping or butter

First cut the lambs' liver into bite-sized pieces, roughly all the same size. Then to make the stuffing, simply combine all the stuffing ingredients together in a bowl and mix thoroughly, with enough milk to bind. Next form the mixture into about 12 balls. Pierce one of them on to a flattened skewer, then thread the meats on (liver, bacon, liver, bacon, then another ball of stuffing and so on), filling 4 skewers. Now brush the kebabs liberally with melted dripping or butter and cook them under a fairly hot grill for about 10 minutes, turning and basting evenly at regular intervals. Serve hot, straight from the grill to the table.

Kidneys with Chipolatas

A cheaper version, this one, of the famous Kidneys Turbigo.

6 lambs' kidneys, skinned, halved and cored
2 level tablespoons butter
2 tablespoons oil
3 slices bread, taken from a large white loaf
6 pork chipolata sausages
1 medium onion, peeled and chopped
½ pint stock
1 level teaspoon dried mustard
1 level teaspoon cornflour
1 teaspoon wine vinegar
½ teaspoon brown sugar
Salt and freshly milled black pepper
A couple of pinches cayenne pepper

First put a serving dish in a warm oven, then heat the butter and oil in a frying pan, and fry the bread slices on both sides until crisp and golden. Then drain the bread slices well on kitchen paper and keep them hot in the oven. Next fry the chipolatas, and keep these warm too. Then cook the kidneys quickly for about 3–4 minutes and arrange them with the chipolatas on the serving dish. Now fry the onion gently until soft and golden and, using a draining spoon, arrange it over the kidneys and sausages. Next add the stock to the pan and boil briskly, scraping the base and sides of the pan, until the stock is reduced by half. Now blend the cornflour, mustard and vinegar in a small basin, stir in the stock, bring to the boil and simmer for 2 or 3 minutes. Sprinkle in the sugar and a couple of pinches of cayenne, taste to check the seasoning, pour the sauce over the kidneys and sausages, and serve.

Liver and Vegetable Hotpot   (Serves 4)

1 lb of ox liver will be plenty for 4 people if you add some bacon
and vegetables and a thick crusty potato topping.

1 lb ox liver
4 oz streaky bacon rashers, rinded
1 carrot, scraped and cut in chunks
1 stick celery, cut in chunks
2 oz swedes, peeled and cut in small chunks
1 tablespoon seasoned flour
3 largish onions, peeled and sliced
1 level teaspoon dried sage
Stock or water
1 teaspoon Worcestershire sauce
2 lb potatoes, peeled and cut into thick slices
A little beef dripping
Salt and freshly milled black pepper

Pre-heat the oven to mark 3/325 °F

Cut the liver into slices about $\frac{1}{4}$ inch thick, then toss the slices
in some seasoned flour. Now in a casserole arrange the slices
of liver, cut vegetables, bacon and onions, seasoning with
pepper, salt and a little dried sage. When everything is in, add
enough stock or water to barely cover the liver etc. (approximately $1-1\frac{1}{4}$ pints), add the Worcester sauce and cover everything with a thick layer of potatoes overlapping each other.
Now add a final sprinkling of salt and pepper, cover closely
and place the casserole in the oven for about $1\frac{1}{2}$ hours. Then
take the lid off, brush the potatoes with a little melted beef
dripping and increase the heat to mark 6/400 °F to let them
get brown and crusty on top—this will take about another
30 minutes.

Liver with Crisp-fried Onions (Serves 4)

Nothing is nicer with liver than some crispy deep-fried onions —and for this recipe, buy the liver from a helpful butcher who'll slice it very thinly for you.

1 lb lambs' liver
2 medium onions, peeled and sliced in thin rings
1 large egg white
2 oz butter
2 tablespoons oil
½ pint beef stock (or potato water)
Seasoned flour
1 level tablespoon flour
Plain flour
Groundnut oil for deep frying
Salt and freshly milled black pepper

The best way to do this is to heat the groundnut oil in a deep-fryer (to 350°) and melt the butter and oil for the liver in a frying pan simultaneously, so that you can cook both the liver and the onions at more or less the same time. Also have some serving dishes keeping warm in the oven with some kitchen paper on them to absorb any excess oil. The liver slices should be coated in seasoned flour and fried quickly over a high heat in the butter and oil (about 1 minute on each side), then kept warm. The onions should be separated into thin rings, dipped first in plain flour, then in stiffly beaten egg white, and deep fried till golden and crisp (for 1 or 2 minutes—it's best to do them a few at a time). Finally sprinkle 1 level tablespoon of flour into the pan juices left from the liver and cook it for a minute or two, then gradually stir in the stock to make a gravy, seasoning well with salt and pepper. Serve the liver garnished with the onions, and the gravy separately.

Kidney Stuffed Onions

(Serves 4)

These are very good served with a very mild flavoured cheese sauce and some savoury rice.

4 large Spanish onions
6 lambs' kidneys, skinned and cored
2 oz butter
2 teaspoons flour
¼ teaspoon dried thyme
4 tablespoons stock
A few drops Worcestershire sauce
Salt and freshly milled pepper
A little extra butter

Peel the onions first, then parboil them in a covered pan with about 1 inch of water in it—give them about 40–45 minutes to half cook. Then drain them and leave them on one side till they are cool enough to handle. Now pre-heat the oven to mark 5/375 °F, carefully remove the centres from the onions (keep them for soups or stews, etc.) and place the onions in a well-buttered gratin dish. Next chop the lambs' kidneys fairly small and fry them in 2 oz of butter for about 5 minutes. Now stir in the flour, cook for a further minute or two and then gradually stir in the stock, a couple of drops of Worcestershire sauce and the thyme. Season well, simmer for a minute or two, then spoon the mixture into the hollowed onions. Add a small knob of butter to each onion and bake in the oven for 30–35 minutes, basting with the juices from time to time.

Oxtail Hotpot

(Serves 3)

1 oxtail, cut into joints
2–3 oz beef dripping
1 small turnip, peeled and cut into chunks
1 small swede, peeled and cut into chunks
2 medium carrots, scraped and cut into chunks
2 sticks celery, cut into chunks
3 small onions, peeled and left whole
1 lb potatoes, peeled and cut into thick slices
1 pint hot water
2 teaspoons Worcestershire sauce
1 heaped tablespoon flour
½ teaspoon dried thyme
1 bayleaf
Salt and freshly milled black pepper
A little extra dripping (melted)

Pre-heat the oven to mark 2/300 °F

In the largest frying pan you have, get the dripping really hot, and quickly brown the pieces of oxtail to a deep brown colour; then transfer them with a draining spoon to a large casserole, season them and sprinkle with thyme. Follow the oxtail with the vegetables (except the potatoes) browning these too just a little, and arrange them all around and over the pieces of oxtail. Add a little more pepper and salt. Now stir the flour into the juices left in the frying pan and allow it to brown before gradually adding the hot water and the Worcestershire sauce. Then transfer the liquid to the casserole (sieving it if it's gone lumpy) and finally arrange the thickly sliced potatoes over the top. Put a lid on and bake for 3 hours, taking the lid off ½ hour before the end, and finally brushing the potatoes with a little melted dripping and browning them until crisp under a hot grill for a few minutes before serving. This dish doesn't really need any extra vegetables to go with it.

Kidneys in Gravy   (Serves 2)

A very quick little casserole for 2 people that can be made in about 30 minutes from start to finish.

6 lambs' kidneys
1 large onion, peeled and chopped
¼ lb dark flat mushrooms
4 rashers unsmoked streaky bacon, rinded and chopped
2 oz dripping or melted kidney fat
½ pint hot water (or potato water)
1 teaspoon Worcestershire sauce
1 heaped teaspoon tomato purée
1 dessertspoon flour
Salt and freshly milled black pepper

Melt the fat in a large saucepan and soften the onion in it for 5 minutes; next add the chopped bacon, cook for another 5 minutes and then add the mushrooms and stir them around for a minute or two. Cut the kidneys into halves, pull off the skins and cut out all the white cores with a pair of scissors. Now turn the heat up under the saucepan, add the kidneys and brown them lightly, stirring them around a bit. Next sprinkle in the flour and stir to soak up the juices. Now stir the tomato purée and Worcestershire sauce into the hot water, then gradually add it to the pan, stirring as you do so. Season with salt and pepper, then put a lid on and simmer very gently for about 20 minutes. Serve with some creamy mashed potato.

Oxtail Braised in Cider

(Serves 4–6)

Alas, oxtail gets more expensive, but it's very plentiful in the autumn and needs some vegetables to eke it out.

$2\frac{1}{2}$–3 lb oxtail, cut into joints
Beef dripping
4 oz streaky bacon, rinded and cut into cubes
2 large onions, peeled and sliced
3 large carrots, scraped and cut in thick chunks
1 oz flour
$\frac{3}{4}$ pint hot beef stock
$\frac{3}{4}$ pint dry cider
1 level teaspoon juniper berries, crushed
1 bayleaf
1 clove garlic, crushed
$\frac{1}{2}$ teaspoon dried thyme
Salt and freshly milled black pepper
Some chopped fresh parsley as a garnish

Pre-heat the oven to mark 2/300 °F

Start by melting the dripping in a large flameproof casserole, get it really hot, then brown the pieces of oxtail, 2 or 3 at a time. Remove them to a plate as they brown, then brown the bacon and chunks of carrot, and remove them to a plate as well. Next fry the onion till browned at the edges. Turn the heat down a bit, then stir in the flour to soak up the juices before gradually adding the stock and cider. Now return the meat, bacon and carrots to the casserole, add the thyme, juniper, garlic and bayleaf, and season with pepper and salt. Put a close-fitting lid on, transfer to the oven and cook for 3 hours. Just before serving, skim off any fat from the surface and sprinkle with fresh chopped parsley.

Liver Casserole

This is a recipe for summer when English lambs' liver is plentiful.

1¼ lb lambs' liver, cut into ¼-inch thick slices
Seasoned flour
1 oz butter
1 tablespoon oil
2 medium onions, peeled and thinly sliced
½ lb new carrots, washed and cut into 1-inch lengths
1 lb tomatoes, skinned and sliced
2 lb small new potatoes, scraped
½ pint stock
½ level teaspoon dried oregano
1 level tablespoon tomato purée
Salt and freshly milled black pepper

Pre-heat the oven to mark 4/350 °F

Begin by drying the liver slices with some kitchen paper, then lightly coat the pieces in well-seasoned flour. Next heat the butter and oil together in a large frying pan and soften the sliced onion in it over a low heat for about 10 minutes. Now arrange half the floured liver slices in the base of a deep oven-proof casserole and cover with a layer of onion, carrots and scraped new potatoes, followed by half the sliced tomatoes. Then repeat all over again, finishing up with a layer of tomatoes. Combine the stock, oregano and tomato purée together in a jug, season, pour this into the casserole, cover closely and bake for approximately 1½ hours, or until the vegetables are tender.

Liver and Onion Yorkshire Pud   (Serves 4)

If you think ½ lb lambs' liver might not be enough for 4 people, try this!

½ lb lambs' liver
1 large onion, peeled and chopped
Some lard

For the batter:
1 egg
4 oz plain flour
¼ pint milk mixed with ¼ pint water
½ teaspoon fresh or dried thyme
Salt and freshly milled black pepper

Pre-heat the oven to mark 7/425 °F

Place a thick-based meat roasting tin (measuring approx. 9 × 6½ inches at the base) on a high shelf in the oven with about 1 oz of lard in it. While it's heating through, make the batter by sifting the flour into a bowl, making a well in the centre of the flour, dropping the egg in and whisking it gradually, incorporating the flour and adding the milk-and-water mixture by degrees until you have a smooth batter. Season it with salt, freshly milled pepper and the thyme. Now cut the liver into thinnish strips about 1 inch in length. Fry the onions in a little more lard to soften them (about 10 minutes), then add the liver and, with the heat fairly high, move it about and turn it to brown nicely—this should take around 2–3 minutes (be careful not to over-cook it). Now take the tin out of the oven, place it over a low heat on top of the stove to keep it sizzling, then spoon in the liver and onions and their juices, and pour the batter over. Return it to the oven and cook for about 35–40 minutes.

Faggots and Peas   (Serves 4)

A real old-fashioned favourite this one, full of flavour and not
too expensive. Caul fat looks like lacey curtains and you can
get it from a good butcher if you order it in advance.

1 lb pig's liver
4 oz green bacon
6 oz pork back fat
(*These first three ingredients should all be cut into 1-inch cubes*)
2 medium onions, peeled
¾ pint stock
2 oz fresh white breadcrumbs
¼ teaspoon dried thyme
¾ teaspoon dried sage
¼ teaspoon powdered mace
About 1 sq yd caul fat
Salt and freshly milled pepper

Then:
1 lb green split peas
1¼ pints chicken stock
1 onion, peeled and quartered
2 oz butter

Pre-heat the oven to mark 4/350 °F

First place the liver, bacon, back fat and onions in a casserole
and pour in the stock. Bake this for 45 minutes, then pour the
contents of the casserole into a large sieve set over a bowl.
Now mince the cooked meats through the fine blade of the
mincer, and mix them with the breadcrumbs, herbs and spice.
Then season well with salt and pepper and form the mixture
into six little cake shapes. Next rinse the caul fat in a bowl of
warm water, drain well and spread it out carefully. Cut out six
6-inch squares, wrap the faggots in them and pack together in a
greased baking dish just big enough to hold them. Now skim
the fat from the stock and pour ½ pint of the stock over the
faggots in the baking dish and bake (uncovered) for about 45
minutes. To cook the peas, put the chicken stock and quartered
onion into a pan and bring to the boil. Add the split peas to the
pan and bring back to the boil, turn down the heat, then cover

and simmer very gently for $1\frac{1}{2}$ hours or until the peas are tender. Then mash with the butter and add salt and pepper to taste (if the mixture is a little dry, add some of the remaining stock from the faggot recipe). Serve the peas with the faggots and the juices poured over.

BANGERS are BEAUTIFUL

Almost every country in the world has some sort of national sausage. I've seen them threaded on skewers over glowing charcoal on the streets of Istanbul and simmering in garlic-laced bean pots in the Tuscan hills, while in France there are dozens of varieties, from the spicy coarse-cut saucissons of Provence to the pale, gutsy andouillets of the Lyonnaise.

In Britain we have bangers. They burst and spread them-selves out over the pan, amalgamating with each other before charring, crisp and black outside and pink and soft within.

Well, they say it takes all sorts, but my complaint is that we really don't have enough sorts: the bran-filled monster I've just described gets awfully boring. Fortunately, we do have a *few* 'beautiful' bangers, made by butchers up and down the country who take a pride in their own particular recipe (my own butcher's are excellent). And if you haven't got a butcher who makes good ones, I suggest you try to get hold of some from Marks & Spencer.

Good sausages, it's true, are more expensive but, because they contain more meat, they don't shrivel and shrink in the cooking, releasing floods of watery fat. Having hunted down the perfect banger, these recipes offered here will help to make them go a bit further (or, if you're prepared to do without skins, you can even make your own).

Homemade Sausages

(Serves 3)

1 lb minced pork (a cheaper cut finely minced)
2 oz shredded beef suet
½ small onion, peeled and grated
2 thick slices bread from a large loaf (crusts off)
1½ tablespoons milk
3 fresh sage leaves, chopped small (or ¼ teaspoon dried)
¼ whole nutmeg, grated
¼ teaspoon chopped thyme (fresh or dried)
1½ tablespoons seasoned flour
Lard
Salt and freshly milled black pepper

Take a large bowl and mix the meat and suet together very thoroughly, then add the grated onion. Soak the bread in the milk, squeeze the excess liquid out, and pop that in too; then mix very thoroughly. Now add the sage, nutmeg, thyme and a good seasoning of salt and freshly milled black pepper. Take care to give it a thorough mixing—it's most important. Next take about a tablespoon of the mixture, press it together, roll it into a sausage shape on a clean surface, then roll it in seasoned flour—and carry on like that until all your sausages are made. To cook, fry them in hot lard to brown all round, then reduce the heat to medium to cook them through. They take about 25 minutes in all. Drain them on crumpled kitchen paper and serve with sauté potatoes and a crisp salad, or with creamy mashed potato, mustard or chutney.

Sausages with Chilli Sauce   (Serves 3)

1 lb pork sausages
1 tablespoon olive oil
1 onion, peeled and chopped
2 cloves garlic, crushed
1 teaspoon dried basil
A 14-oz tin Italian tomatoes
1 whole dried red chilli (or ¼ teaspoon chilli powder)
¼ teaspoon sugar
1 teaspoon tomato purée
1 small green pepper, de-seeded and diced
Salt and freshly milled black pepper

Begin by de-seeding the chilli (if you are using a whole one),
discarding the fiery seeds and chopping the red part finely. Now
heat the olive oil in a flameproof casserole or saucepan, brown
the sausages all round and, using a draining spoon, remove
them from the pan. Next stir the onion, green pepper and garlic
into the fat remaining in the pan and cook gently until softened
(about 10 minutes). Now stir in the remaining ingredients,
bring up to simmering point, then return the sausages to the
pan. Allow it to simmer very gently (uncovered), stirring
occasionally, for about 25 minutes until the tomatoes are reduced to a thick sauce-like consistency. Then taste and season
with salt and pepper before serving. This is very good served
with buttered noodles or creamy mashed potato.

Sausage Stuffed Onions   (Serves 4)

If you can, try to get the very largest (preferably Spanish)
onions for this.

4 large Spanish onions
½ lb good sausagemeat
2 oz mushrooms, finely chopped
1½ oz butter

½ teaspoon dried sage
1 oz dry white breadcrumbs
2 tablespoons chopped fresh parsley
A 5-oz carton yoghurt
1 small cooking apple, peeled, cored and chopped
1 clove garlic, crushed
Paprika
Salt and freshly milled black pepper
A little extra butter

Pre-heat the oven to mark 6/400 °F

After you've peeled the onions, put them in a large pan of boiling salted water. Bring the water back to the boil, cover and simmer gently for about 30 minutes. Then drain the onions and leave them to cool. Now cut a thin cap from the top of each onion and scoop out the centres, leaving a fairly substantial shell. Arrange the onion cases (packing them closely together) in a deep, buttered baking dish. Then chop up the onion you removed. Next heat 1½ oz of butter in a frying pan and measure 3 tablespoons of the chopped onion into it. Fry briskly for a minute or two before adding the sausagemeat and sage—mashing it down with a fork until separate and evenly coloured. Then stir in the garlic, mushrooms, breadcrumbs and apple. Taste and season with salt and pepper (some sausagemeats come quite highly seasoned to start with, so do taste it first). Now remove the pan from the heat and stir in a tablespoon of yoghurt together with the parsley. Put the mixture into the onion shells—if it seems a little too much, just pile it up on top. Then transfer the baking dish to the top half of the oven and bake for 20 minutes. Finally put a blob of yoghurt on each onion and dust with paprika. Replace in the oven for a further 5–10 minutes and serve with creamy mashed potato.

Note: Any bits of onion centres left over can be used for soups or stocks.

Frankfurters with Hot Potato Salad   (Serves 4)

If you have a delicatessen in your area, try to get the really long frankfurters for this recipe, as they're generally much better than the supermarket variety.

8 large frankfurters
1½ lb potatoes
1 medium onion, peeled, halved and thinly sliced
6 tablespoons oil
2 tablespoons cider vinegar
1 teaspoon made mustard
A few drops tabasco
2 tablespoons chopped fresh parsley
1 clove garlic, crushed
Salt and freshly milled black pepper

To start with, scrub the potatoes well (but don't peel them), then boil them in salted water until they're just tender. While that's happening, heat 2 tablespoons of oil in a separate pan and fry the onion and crushed garlic for 2 or 3 minutes. Then add the remaining oil and the cider vinegar, stir in the mustard, tabasco, salt and freshly milled pepper, and heat until boiling. Then turn the heat low and, at this stage, poach the frankfurters (but check with the supplier for how long, because it does vary). Next drain the boiled potatoes, put them in a warm serving bowl and pour over the hot oil and vinegar mixture. Now sprinkle with the parsley and, using a sharp knife, roughly chop the potatoes. Then serve with the hot cooked frankfurters on top, and have some extra mustard on the table.

Note: I always like to leave the skins on the potatoes, but if you like you can peel them off as soon as the potatoes are drained.

Bangers Braised in Cider

(Serves 3)

I always use herb-flavoured sausages for this, but any sort of pork sausages will do.

1 lb pork sausages
½ lb lean streaky bacon in one piece (then cut into cubes)
½ lb small button onions, peeled
½ teaspoon dried thyme
1 bayleaf
1 clove garlic, crushed
1 heaped teaspoon flour
1 Cox's apple, cored and cut into rings (no need to peel it)
½ pint dry cider
Lard
A little butter
Salt and freshly milled black pepper

Pre-heat the oven to mark 4/350 °F

Take a large flameproof casserole, melt a little lard in it and brown the sausages all round. Then, using a slotted spoon, remove them to a plate whilst you brown the bacon cubes and onion lightly. When they're done, sprinkle in a heaped tea-spoon of flour to soak up the juices, then gradually stir in the cider. Now pop the sausages back in, plus the garlic, bayleaf and thyme and a little seasoning; put a lid on when it all comes to simmering point and then transfer to the oven for 30 minutes. When the 30 minutes is up, remove the lid and cook for a fur-ther 20–30 minutes. Before serving, fry the apple rings in butter until soft and garnish the casserole with them. This is lovely served with spicy red cabbage.

Toad-in-the-Hole with Sage and Onions   (Serves 4)

Not an attractive name, admittedly, but it's a delicious classic, especially if you make it with good-quality pork sausages, a little sage and fried onion rings.

1 lb pure pork sausages
2 medium onions, peeled and sliced thinly
1 level teaspoon dried sage
2 large eggs
6 oz plain flour
6 fl. oz milk
4 fl. oz water
Beef dripping or lard
Salt and freshly milled black pepper

Pre-heat the oven to mark 7/425 °F

First put a tablespoon of dripping into a solid-based roasting tin (base measuring about 9 × 7 inches) and pop it into the oven to heat. Then in a frying pan melt some more fat and brown the onions for about 5 minutes or so until they have softened a bit. Remove them to a plate and lightly brown the sausages all round—again for about 5 minutes. While they're browning, make the batter by sifting the flour into a bowl. Make a well in the middle, drop the eggs in and, using an electric hand-whisk (or a fork), whisk the eggs, incorporating the flour and adding the milk and water mixed together first. Season the batter with salt, pepper and sage. When the fat in the tin starts to sizzle, take it out of the oven and keep it sizzling by placing it on top of the stove over a medium heat. Then put in the sausages and the onions on top of them and, making sure the fat is still very hot, pour in the batter. Quickly shake the tin to get the batter all round the base of the sausages etc., then transfer the tin back to the highest shelf of the oven and let it bake for about 40 minutes, or until puffy and crisp. Serve straightaway, with gravy or apple and onion sauce.

Sausages with Lentils (Serves 4)

1½ lb sausages
6 oz dried green lentils (not the orange ones)
1 level tablespoon butter
1 tablespoon oil
1 large onion, peeled and chopped
2 cloves garlic, crushed
A 15-oz can Italian tomatoes
1 bayleaf
2 or 3 pinches thyme
1 level teaspoon sugar
A little extra oil
Salt and freshly milled black pepper

Rinse the lentils, place them in a saucepan with enough water
to cover (don't add any salt), bring them to simmering point
and simmer gently for about 30 minutes, or until the lentils
are tender but not disintegrating. Now drain them, and keep
the cooking liquid. Then fry the onion and garlic in the butter
and oil, add the tinned tomatoes, sugar, thyme and bayleaf,
and let it all simmer gently (without a lid) until the liquid
reduces and it becomes rather thick—you may need to stir it
now and then. Now in a frying pan brown the sausages all
over in a little oil. Then, using a draining spoon, transfer them
to the tomato mixture. Add the lentils now and approximately
½ pint of the liquid they were cooked in. Stir well, then continue cooking over a very gentle heat for about 30 minutes—
again without a lid, and if the mixture begins to look dry add a
little more liquid. Taste and add pepper and salt, if it needs it,
before serving.

Pork Sausages with Cider Sauce

I first made this using red wine, but now I've switched to cider and it's every bit as good.

1 oz lard
1 lb good-quality pork sausages
1 onion, peeled and chopped
4 slices streaky bacon, rinded and chopped
2 level teaspoons flour
4 oz dark mushrooms, sliced
4 fl. oz dry cider
¼ pint stock or water
¼ teaspoon dried thyme
2 teaspoons tomato purée
1 teaspoon redcurrant jelly
Salt and freshly milled black pepper

First gently brown the sausages all over in the lard, then using a draining spoon transfer them to a plate and keep them on one side. Now add the onion and the bacon to the fat remaining in the pan and cook these for about 10 minutes, or until the onion is soft. Then sprinkle in the flour and stir it round to soak up the juices; add the mushrooms and cook for 5 more minutes before stirring in the cider and stock. Next add the tomato purée, thyme and redcurrant jelly, bring to simmering point, taste and season and cook gently without a cover for about 15 minutes. These are delicious served with some creamy mashed potatoes or even some onion-flavoured rice.

Sausages Boulangère

(Serves 3)

These are nice served with some freshly made sharp English mustard.

1 lb sausages
1½ lb potatoes, peeled and very thinly sliced
1 medium onion, peeled and finely chopped
¼ pint milk
¼ pint stock or water
A little oil
1 teaspoon dried mixed herbs
1 oz butter
Salt and freshly milled black pepper

Pre-heat the oven to mark 4/350°F

Brown the sausages all over in a little oil in a frying pan—this should take around 5 or 6 minutes—and while that's happening put a smear of butter round the base of a casserole. Then put in a layer of the potatoes, a sprinkling of onion and seasoning, and repeat the layers until all the potatoes are in, finishing off with a few flecks of butter. Now remove the browned sausages from the pan, using a draining spoon, and place these on top of the potatoes. Sprinkle in the dried herbs, pour in the milk and water, cover the casserole with a piece of foil, place it in the oven and bake for about 45 minutes. Then remove the foil and bake for a further 15–20 minutes, or until the potatoes are tender when tested with a thin skewer.

Purée of Peas with Sausages (Serves 3)

This makes a nice accompaniment to 1 lb of ordinary fried sausages.

1 lb green split peas
1 small onion, peeled and stuck with 4 cloves
¼ teaspoon mixed herbs
4 tablespoons cream
1 oz butter
Salt and freshly milled black pepper
Freshly grated nutmeg

Put the split peas in a pan and cover them with cold water. Bring this to the boil very slowly, remove from the heat and leave to soak for 1 hour. Then drain the peas and place them back in the saucepan together with the onion stuck with cloves, the mixed herbs and some salt. Cover again with cold water and simmer till tender (about 20 minutes). Then drain the peas again and rub them through a sieve into the top of a double saucepan (or a basin sitting over some simmering water); stir in the cream and butter, and leave it like this for about 20 minutes, stirring now and then until it becomes very thick. Season with pepper and freshly grated nutmeg, and more salt if it needs it. Serve the purée piled on to a plate with the fried sausages on top.

Poor Man's Cassoulet (Serves 4)

This is a much cheaper and easier version than the original classic Cassoulet. Nevertheless, do try to get decent bangers if possible.

¾ lb long haricot beans (available at healthfood shops and
  delicatessens)
1 lb pork sausages
½ lb streaky bacon, bought in one piece then cut into cubes
1½ tablespoons tomato purée
¾ level teaspoon dried thyme
4 oz breadcrumbs
3 medium onions, peeled and sliced
3 cloves garlic, finely chopped
Groundnut oil
Salt and freshly milled black pepper

Pre-heat the oven to mark 1/275 °F

Either soak the beans overnight or wash them, place them in a saucepan, cover with plenty of cold water, bring to the boil and let them boil for 1 minute. Then turn out the heat and let them soak for 2–3 hours. Then in a flameproof casserole, heat some oil and brown the sausages to a nice golden colour. Remove them to a plate, then colour the bacon cubes a little and transfer them to join the waiting sausages. Now in the juices left in the pan soften the onion and garlic for 10 minutes, and while that's happening drain the beans (reserving their soaking water). Put a layer of beans into the cooking pot containing the onion and garlic, then add half the sausages and bacon, followed by more beans, the rest of the sausages and bacon, and finally the rest of the beans. Next measure 1¼ pints of the soaking water, stir 1½ tablespoons of tomato purée into it along with the thyme and a seasoning of salt and pepper—but be sparing with the salt (because of the bacon). Pour this over the rest of the ingredients, then cover and bake for 2 hours. Then take the lid off, sprinkle the breadcrumbs all over the top, and bake (without a lid) for a further hour. This is very rich and hefty, so a green salad is really all it needs to go with it.

COOK FOR VICTORY

1976 must surely go down as the year Britain took to the spade. Was it the potato crisis, the exorbitant prices or the media jumping on another bandwagon? Where once the bookshelves were dominated by cookery books, there are now an equal number of baffling and bewildering gardening books and step-by-step part-works with titles like *Grow It and Cook It, Grow It and Freeze It*.

Very commendable, and I hope the harvest proves worth all the sweat, because for too long (while meat was plentiful) vegetables have played a secondary role, just a little something to help the meat go down. I believe this is changing now, if only because we've travelled abroad more and been made more aware of the full potential of vegetables—that what might have been a simple uninspiring meal can be transformed into something much more special by the clever treatment of vegetables.

Take marrow, one of our cheapest and most easily grown vegetables yet so often relegated to a watery white sauce. Try it on its own with tomatoes, garlic and crushed coriander seeds, and see what I mean. If you grow fresh herbs, then do make some herb butter (by chopping up a mixture of herbs and combining them with butter) and just swirl a knob of this around cooked new potatoes or carrots or cauliflower—it instantly puts them into the four-star bracket. All the recipes here attempt to make the most of vegetables, whether they're to be eaten on their own or used to jazz up cold meat, sausages or other fairly simple dishes.

Broad Bean Salad

(Serves 2)

1½ lb broad beans (that is, 1½ lb before shelling)
1 rasher lean bacon, rinded
1 tablespoon fresh chopped herbs (I use a mixture of
    tarragon, marjoram and parsley)
4 spring onions, finely chopped

For the dressing:
½ clove garlic, crushed
1 teaspoon English mustard powder
1 dessertspoon lemon juice
1 dessertspoon wine vinegar
1 level teaspoon crushed rock salt
Freshly milled black pepper
4 dessertspoons oil

First cook the bacon until it's really crisp, then drain it well
and crumble it into very small pieces. Next make the dressing
by dissolving the salt in the lemon juice and vinegar for ½ hour,
then shake it with the rest of the ingredients in a screw-top
jar to get everything thoroughly amalgamated. Now cook the
shelled beans in a very little salted water for about 5 minutes—
it's very important not to overcook them or they'll lose their
colour and go mushy—then drain them thoroughly and toss
them in the dressing while they're still warm. When they're
cool, toss in the finely chopped spring onion and bacon, and
serve the salad on some crisp lettuce leaves.

Baked Aubergines

(Serves 4)

Aubergines done like this go extremely well with lamb, or they're good on their own as a lunch-time dish with lots of fresh bread and perhaps a green salad.

4 aubergines (about 1¾ lb)
4 tablespoons oil
1 large onion, peeled and finely chopped
6 fairly large tomatoes, skinned and chopped
2 cloves garlic, crushed
2 tablespoons finely chopped fresh parsley
A very generous pinch each ground allspice, cinnamon and
    caster sugar
Salt and freshly milled black pepper
A little butter

For the topping:
2–3 tablespoons dry white breadcrumbs
1 tablespoon grated Parmesan or other cheese
1 tablespoon butter

First cut the aubergines into smallish pieces, then place them in a colander and sprinkle with 2 heaped teaspoons of salt. Put a plate on top of them with a weight on it and leave them to drain for an hour. Then, when you're ready to cook them, pre-heat the oven to mark 5/375 °F and well butter a shallow baking dish. Drain and dry the aubergines as thoroughly as possible on kitchen paper, then heat the oil in a frying pan. When it's hot, add the aubergines to the pan and fry them until they're a pale golden colour. Now add the onion to the pan and continue cooking until it has softened slightly; then add the prepared tomatoes, crushed garlic and parsley, and season with the spices, caster sugar, salt and pepper. Simmer gently now, stirring a bit, for about 5 minutes. Next transfer the mixture to the baking dish, sprinkle the top with a mixture of cheese and breadcrumbs, and dot the surface with the butter. Then bake near the top of the oven for about 30 minutes, or until bubbling and browned on top.

Tomato and Chilli Sauce

(Serves 2)

¾ lb red, ripe tomatoes, skinned
1 small onion, peeled and finely chopped
1 clove garlic, crushed
1 teaspoon tomato purée
1 teaspoon dried basil
¼ teaspoon chilli powder
1 tablespoon olive oil
Salt and freshly milled black pepper

To skin the tomatoes, pour boiling water over them, leave for 1 minute, then put them in cold water and slip the skins off. Now halve them and chop the flesh quite small. Next soften the onion and garlic in a saucepan with the olive oil, then add the tomatoes, tomato purée, the basil and chilli powder, and season with salt. Stir well, simmer gently for 15 minutes with the lid on and then for a further 10 or 15 minutes without the lid. When it's ready, taste to check the seasoning, then either sieve the mixture or blend it in a liquidiser, or else serve it just as it is.

White Cabbage with Garlic and Coriander

(Serves 4)

Cooking vegetables in the oven is only economical if the oven is on anyway, so try to cook this dish when you are using the oven for something else.

1 small white cabbage, weighing about 1½ lb
2 tablespoons groundnut oil
1 heaped teaspoon crushed coriander seed
1 arge clove garlic, crushed
Salt and freshly milled black pepper

First take away any stale or tough outer leaves from the cabbage, then using a sharp knife cut it into quarters and remove the tough stalky bits. Now, leaving the quarters intact, wash them and then dry them as thoroughly as possible. Pour the oil over the base of the casserole, add the crushed garlic and put it into the oven to heat through—the temperature should be mark 4/350 °F. Meanwhile crush the coriander seed, preferably in a pestle and mortar but failing that you can use a small basin and the end of a rolling pin. When the oil is hot and beginning to sizzle, add the crushed coriander seed, then the pieces of cabbage. Baste each piece a little, season with salt and pepper, put a lid on the casserole and put it back in the oven for about 40 minutes, or until the cabbage is tender when tested with a skewer.

Turnips Boulangère

(Serves 6)

Potatoes Boulangère are quite well known, but in fact this method works particularly well with turnips too.

2 lb small (tender) turnips
1 onion, peeled and finely chopped
2 slices streaky bacon, rinded and chopped small
¼ pint hot stock
¼ pint milk

1 oz of butter
Some extra butter
Salt and freshly milled black pepper

Pre-heat the oven to mark 4/350 °F

First peel the turnips and slice them as thinly as possible. Then arrange the ingredients in a 4½-pint casserole or baking dish (generously buttered) as follows: a layer of sliced turnips in the base, followed by a sprinkling of onion and a seasoning of salt and pepper. Continue with another layer of turnips, then onion and so on until everything is in and you've finished up with a layer of turnips on top. Now pour in the milk and hot stock, season once again, and dot the surface with the 1 oz of butter. Finally, sprinkle the chopped bacon over the top and cover it all with a sheet of buttered foil. Bake in the top half of the oven for an hour. After that time remove the foil, and bake for a further 30 minutes—or until the turnips feel soft when tested with a skewer

Mashed Swede with Bacon (Serves 6)

2 lb swedes
4 rashers streaky bacon, rinded and chopped small
2 oz butter
2 tablespoons milk
Salt and freshly milled black pepper

Peel the swedes, cut them into smallish cubes, place them in a saucepan and pour over enough boiling water to just cover them. Add some salt and simmer for about 20–30 minutes, or until the cubes are tender. Now pour the swede into a colander to drain thoroughly and return the saucepan to the heat, add a knob of butter and then quickly fry the chopped bacon until it's just beginning to crisp. Next return the swede to the saucepan and mash to a creamy pulp, adding the rest of the butter and 2 tablespoons of milk. Season well with salt and freshly milled black pepper, and serve piled on to a warm serving dish.

147

Courgettes à la Grecque (Serves 2)

If you decide to grow courgettes they'll come at you at such a rate that you'll be wondering what on earth to do with them next. So here's another idea.

¾ lb small courgettes
1 medium-sized onion, peeled and chopped small
1 clove garlic, crushed
1 tablespoon wine vinegar
6 tablespoons water
1 large tomato, skinned and chopped
½ teaspoon oregano
1 tablespoon chopped fresh parsley
6 coriander seeds, lightly crushed
6 black peppercorns, lightly crushed
3 tablespoons oil
Juice of 1 small lemon
Salt

First heat 2 tablespoons of oil in a heavy pan and soften the onion and garlic in it gently for about 10 minutes. Then add the wine vinegar, 6 tablespoons water, the crushed coriander and peppercorns, oregano, the lemon juice and a little salt. Bring to the boil and simmer for 5 minutes. Then prepare the courgettes: don't peel them, just wipe them, trim off the ends and cut into 1-inch slices. Add them to the sauce together with the chopped tomato, stir, put the lid on and simmer over a gentle heat for about 20 minutes, or until they're tender. Now transfer the lot to a serving dish, allow to cool, then cover and chill. Just before serving sprinkle with 1 more tablespoon of oil and some fresh chopped parsley. Then all it needs is some crusty fresh bread.

Purée of Parsnips

(Serves 4)

If you make this in January or February, when parsnips are really cheap, then I think a ¼ pint of cream will be justified.

1 lb parsnips
¾ pint hot water
¼ pint single cream
Freshly grated nutmeg
Salt and freshly milled black pepper

First peel the parsnips, discard any of the woody centre bits and chop them up into small cubes. Now bring the water up to boiling point in a saucepan, add the cubed parsnips, bring them back to simmering point, cover and cook for about 10 minutes, or until tender. Then drain them, reserving their cooking liquid. Next, either tip them into a liquidiser and blend them to a purée with the cream or sieve them, beating the cream in with a fork bit by bit. Either way, taste and season with freshly grated nutmeg, salt and pepper, adding 1 or 2 tablespoons of their cooking liquid, if you think it needs it.

Marrow with Tomatoes and Coriander

(Serves 4)

A 1½-lb marrow (a young one will be smallish, have a shiny skin, and when you press one of the ridges with your thumb it will leave an impression)

½ lb red ripe tomatoes (about 4 medium), skinned and chopped

½ medium onion, peeled and chopped

1 clove garlic, crushed

¾ teaspoon whole coriander seeds

1 dessertspoon fresh chopped basil (or 1 level teaspoon of dried)

Oil

Salt and freshly milled black pepper

Pre-heat the oven to mark 3/325°F

In a flameproof casserole melt about a tablespoon of oil, add the onion and crushed garlic, and soften it for about 5 minutes; then stir in the chopped tomatoes and cook for a further 5 minutes. If the marrow is fresh it won't need peeling; simply cut it into 1½-inch (approx.) chunks and add them to the tomatoes and onions along with the coriander seeds (crushed first with a pestle and mortar or with the back of a tablespoon). Then add the basil, and season with salt and pepper. Stir everything around well, put a lid on and place the casserole in the oven to cook for about 1 hour. About 10 minutes before the end of the cooking time, put the casserole back on the top of the stove and simmer without a lid to reduce some of the liquid.

Note: This tastes good even cold or re-heated the next day.

New Potatoes with Bacon and Onion

(Serves 3)

Serve this with fresh fried eggs and you have a very quick and simple supper dish.

1½ lb new potatoes, scrubbed but not peeled
1 oz butter
1 tablespoon oil
6 slices bacon, rinded and cut into strips
1 large onion, peeled and chopped small
1 clove garlic, crushed
Salt and freshly milled black pepper

First of all slice the potatoes into rounds no more than about ¼ inch thick. Then melt the butter and oil in a large heavy frying pan, and fry the bacon strips, chopped onion and crushed garlic over a gentle heat until just softened. Now add the sliced potatoes to the pan, season with salt and freshly milled black pepper, give it all a really good stir around, then cover with a well-fitting lid (a heatproof plate will do if you've no lid) and leave to cook very gently for about 20–25 minutes, or until the potato slices are tender. Stir once or twice during the cooking to make sure that the heat is not too high and that the potatoes are not sticking to the base of the pan. When they're ready, spoon them into a heatproof serving dish and serve with fried eggs on top.

Soufflé'd Jacket Potatoes

4 large potatoes baked in their jackets
2 oz butter
1 carton soured cream or yoghurt
6–8 spring onions, finely chopped
3 eggs, separated
1 tablespoon chopped parsley
Salt and freshly milled black pepper

Pre-heat the oven to mark 6/400 °F

Bake the potatoes. Then as soon as they're cooked, remove them from the oven, leaving the heat at mark 6/400 °F, then (with your hands in oven gloves, or using a teacloth for protection) cut the potatoes in half and scoop out the centres into a bowl. Next arrange the potato shells in a shallow roasting tin (using one potato to prop up another if they don't sit comfortably straight). Now melt the butter in a saucepan and fry the spring onions for 2–3 minutes; then add all the onion and melted butter to the potato together with the soured cream and egg yolks, and whisk (preferably with an electric hand-whisk) until smooth. Taste and season well with salt and pepper and add the parsley. Now, with a clean whisk, beat the egg whites until stiff and carefully fold them into the potato mixture. Pile the mixture back into the potato shells and return them to the top half of the oven for 15–20 minutes, or until puffed and golden brown on top. Serve immediately—with some homemade chutney to dip the skins in.

Irish Potatoes

(Serves 4–6)

This is an excellent way to jazz up potatoes, especially for serving with cold leftover meat.

2 lb potatoes
½ lb green cabbage, shredded
1 bunch spring onions, chopped
2 oz butter, meat dripping or bacon fat
2 tablespoons cream (or top of the milk)
Salt and freshly milled black pepper

Put a kettle on to boil while you peel the potatoes and cut them into even-sized pieces. Then place them in a saucepan, add salt, pour over enough boiling water to just cover them, and simmer until tender. Meanwhile place the washed cabbage in a saucepan, add salt and pour boiling water on that too. When it comes to the boil, cook it for 5 minutes, then drain very thoroughly in a colander, pressing out all the excess liquid very carefully. Now return the saucepan to the heat, melt the fat in it and add the spring onions and drained cabbage. Stir them around, keeping the heat very low. Then put a lid on and let them sweat gently without browning for 10 minutes. While that's happening, drain the potatoes, add some pepper and whip them to a purée with the cream or milk (an electric hand-whisk will do this in seconds). Now add the onion and cabbage and their juices, combine them with the potato and serve very hot.

Old-fashioned Bubble and Squeak

(Serves 2)

It's funny how some very humble dishes like this one can be very special simply because of their rarity—so here's to a comeback for good old Bubble and Squeak!

1 lb potatoes, peeled
1 small cabbage
1 heaped tablespoon well-seasoned flour
1 oz butter
Salt and freshly milled black pepper
Some good beef dripping for frying

Put the potatoes on to cook in some salted boiling water, then half fill a medium-sized saucepan with some more salted water and bring it to the boil. Cut the cabbage into quarters, remove the hard stalk and shred the rest. Wash it thoroughly, then plunge it into the fast-boiling water, put a lid on and let it boil for about 6 minutes. Now pour it into a colander, put a plate (one that fits inside the colander) on top of the cabbage, place a weight on top and leave it to drain very thoroughly. When the potatoes are cooked, add some pepper and a knob of butter. Mash them (with an electric hand-mixer if you have one) until smooth—don't add any milk, though, because you don't want them to be too soft. Now mix the well-drained cabbage into the potato, and when it is cool take tablespoons of the mixture and shape them into round cakes, which should then be dusted in the seasoned flour. Fry them in hot dripping to a good, crisp, golden brown on both sides. Drain on crumpled grease-proof paper and serve immediately.

Note: You can, of course, make this with leftover potatoes and cabbage or sprouts; also a little chopped fried onion is a nice addition.

GO WITH THE GRAIN

It is a fact of life—established by the charts and graphs of the British Nutrition Foundation—that as our affluence increases, so our cereal consumption decreases. And the same is true in reverse, of course. But whatever our economic condition, grains in all their forms are obviously very important (one need hardly mention that they are the staple food of two-thirds of the world).

I've always had great admiration for the way the Italians, for instance, manage to stretch out their meagre meat rations with the most delicate dishes of pasta. In fact, our household is hooked on it, and we have it regularly once a week. I have investigated *making* pasta at home, but it is quite a strenuous and lengthy exercise and, at the time of writing, doesn't seem to me all that much of a saving (so I haven't included it here). But bear in mind, when you're buying pasta, that a pound of it serves 4 people—so it really is economical.

Some people still feel nervous about cooking rice. However, if you follow the instructions I've given here, you won't ever have any trouble. Don't, whatever you do, buy the so-called 'easy-cook' rice. It's much more expensive, and as all rice is easy to cook once it has been explained, you'll have wasted your money!

Onion Rice
(Serves 3–4)

Cooking rice needn't be a problem if a few simple rules are followed. The first rule is always buy good-quality long-grain rice; the second is it's better to measure rice and liquid by volume rather than by weight; and, most important of all, don't keep opening the cooking pot and giving the rice hefty stirs, because this will break the grains, release the starch and cause the rice to become soggy. Don't stir it at all during the cooking, just wait until all the liquid has been absorbed, then tip the rice into a serving dish and fluff it *gently* with a fork.

1 teacup long-grain rice
2½ teacups hot stock or water
1 oz butter
1 tablespoon groundnut oil
½ medium onion, peeled and finely chopped
½ level teaspoon salt
Freshly milled black pepper

Begin by melting the butter and oil in a thick-based saucepan and gently cooking the onions in it for about 5 minutes. Then add the rice and stir it around with a wooden spoon so that it gets a nice coating of butter. Now pour in the hot chicken stock and add some seasoning. Stir just once, and when it reaches boiling point put a lid on and simmer gently for 20–25 minutes, or until all the liquid is absorbed and the rice is tender. Empty the rice into a serving dish and fluff the grains with a fork to separate them.

Onion Rice with Herbs This can be cooked as above, adding ½ teaspoon of dried mixed herbs or 1 teaspoon of chopped fresh herbs.

Spiced Pilau Rice Again, cook as above, adding with the rice 2 whole cloves, a 1½-inch piece of cinnamon stick and 1 teaspoon of powdered turmeric.

With all the above methods, if you use brown rice you'll need 40 minutes cooking time and to use slightly less liquid, as in the following recipe.

Brown Rice Salad

(Serves 4)

1 teacup or mug long-grain brown rice
1¾ teacups boiling water
3 or 4 tablespoons vinaigrette dressing (see p. 143)
3 spring onions, very finely chopped
2 inches cucumber, finely chopped
2 large tomatoes, skinned and finely chopped
½ red or green pepper, de-seeded and finely chopped
1 red dessert apple, chopped but not peeled
1 oz currants
1 oz walnuts, finely chopped
Salt and freshly milled black pepper

Place the rice and some salt in a saucepan, pour the boiling water over and bring it back to the boil; then stir once, put a lid on and simmer very gently for 40 minutes or so until all the liquid has been absorbed. Now empty the rice into a salad bowl, fluff it up with a fork and pour the dressing over while it's still hot. Allow it to cool and then mix in all the other ingredients, adding a little more dressing it if needs it and tasting to check the seasoning. Keep in a cool place until needed.

Brown Rice with Vegetables   (Serves 2)

Serve this with some good cheese and crusty bread to follow
and I promise you won't miss the meat.

2 tablespoons butter
2 tablespoons oil
1 large green pepper, de-seeded and chopped
1 medium onion, peeled and roughly chopped
2 sticks celery, chopped
1 teacup long-grain brown rice
3 oz mushrooms, sliced
2 teacups boiling stock (or water)
½ teaspoon dried thyme
3 tablespoons chopped parsley
6 spring onions, finely chopped (including green parts)
Salt and freshly milled black pepper

First heat the butter and oil in a large, solid saucepan, then
add the prepared peppers, onion and celery to the pan and
cook them over a *fairly* low heat until they're softened and
slightly golden. Now put the rice in a sieve and rinse well with
cold water. Drain it, shaking any excess water out, and add it
to the saucepan, with the sliced mushrooms, stirring well.
Cook for a minute or two before pouring in the stock. Add the
thyme, season with salt and pepper, and bring to simmering
point; then cover and cook very gently for about 35–40
minutes, or until the rice is just tender. As soon as the rice
seems to be *almost* cooked, remove the lid from the pan and
continue to cook until the rice is tender and free from any
liquid. Then sprinkle in the parsley and the chopped spring
onions. Taste and season with more salt and pepper if
necessary.

Buttered Noodles with Meat Balls

(Serves 4)

Serve these delicious little meat balls with ribbon noodles or spaghetti.

1 lb ribbon noodles (or spaghetti)
Salt
A little oil
Butter

For the Meat Balls:
A ½-inch thick slice of white bread with the crusts removed
3 or 4 tablespoons milk
½ lb minced beef
½ lb minced pork
1 small onion, peeled and finely chopped
2 tablespoons chopped parsley
¼ teaspoon dried thyme
¼ teaspoon freshly grated nutmeg
1 teaspoon salt
Freshly milled black pepper
1 egg, beaten
Seasoned flour
Oil for frying

For the sauce:
A 14-oz tin Italian tomatoes
1 small onion, peeled and finely chopped
1 clove garlic, crushed
1 teaspoon dried basil
1 tablespoon oil
Seasoning

To make the sauce, soften the onion and garlic in the oil in a pan, then add the tomatoes, basil and seasoning and simmer without a lid for about 20 minutes. While it cooks, soak the bread in the milk for a few minutes, then squeeze out the milk and shred the bread into a large bowl. Mix the bread, minced meats, chopped onion, herbs and spices together with the beaten egg; form the mixture into meat balls a bit larger in

160

size than a walnut—you'll find the mixture makes about 16. Roll the balls in seasoned flour, then heat some oil in a large frying pan and fry the meat balls in the hot fat until they are browned and cooked through (about 8–10 minutes). Boil the ribbon noodles (or spaghetti) in salted water with a few drops of oil added for 12 minutes. Then drain the meat balls well and keep them warm. Drain the ribbon noodles, toss them in butter, and serve them with the meat balls and the sauce.

Spaghetti Bolognese

(Serves 4)

For the Ragu Bolognese:
3 oz chicken livers, chopped small
6 oz lean minced beef
2 rashers streaky bacon (unsmoked), finely chopped
1 teaspoon dried basil
1 small onion, peeled and very finely chopped
An 8-oz tin of Italian tomatoes
1 fat clove garlic, crushed
4 tablespoons red wine
2 heaped tablespoons tomato purée
1½ tablespoons olive oil

And then:
1 lb spaghetti
1 oz butter
Some Parmesan cheese, grated
Salt and freshly milled black pepper

Begin by making the ragu: heat the olive oil in a thick-based saucepan and in it gently soften the onions, chopped bacon and garlic for 5 minutes. Turning the heat up, add the chicken livers together with the beef to brown (keeping everything on the move with a wooden spoon). When the meat has browned, add the contents of the tin of tomatoes along with the basil, red wine and tomato purée, and some seasoning, cover the saucepan and simmer gently for 20 minutes. After that time take off the lid and continue simmering gently for a further

20–25 minutes, so that the sauce can get nicely concentrated. Towards the end of this cooking time, fill a large saucepan with water, bring to the boil, add some salt and then the spaghetti (if you also add about a teaspoon of olive oil to the water, this will help prevent the pasta sticking together). When the spaghetti has sunk down into the water, stir thoroughly, then cover and simmer very gently for 12 minutes. Strain the cooked spaghetti in a warmed colander, add a knob of butter and a few twists of freshly milled pepper, then transfer on to warmed plates. Pour the sauce over and serve with grated Parmesan sprinkled over.

Spaghetti with Tuna and Olives   (Serves 3)

A 7½-oz can tuna in oil
1 large onion, peeled and chopped
4 oz button mushrooms, quartered
1 lb ripe tomatoes, skinned and chopped
1 tablespoon tomato purée
1 clove garlic, crushed
1 teaspoon dried basil
2 oz green stuffed olives, chopped
1 lb spaghetti
Salt and freshly milled black pepper
A little butter
Some grated Parmesan cheese

First drain the oil from the tin of tuna into a saucepan, heat it gently and fry the onion and garlic until softened. Then add the mushrooms to the pan and cook for a further 2 or 3 minutes. Now pour the tomatoes into the pan, add the tuna, tomato purée and basil, then cover and cook for a further 10–15 minutes, or until the mixture has reduced to a nice consistency. Next add the olives, taste, and season with salt and pepper. Cook the spaghetti for 10–12 minutes in plenty of salted water, drain and toss a little butter in. Then season well with salt and pepper, and serve the spaghetti topped with the sauce and have some freshly grated Parmesan to go with it.

162

Macaroni Carbonara (Serves 2)

I find this recipe indispensable for a delicious spur-of-the-moment meal that can be conjured up from ingredients I nearly always have in the house.

½ lb any supermarket macaroni
4 oz streaky bacon, chopped
2 large eggs
2 tablespoons grated Parmesan cheese
A knob of butter
A little oil
Salt and freshly milled black pepper

Before you cook the macaroni, have ready a large mixing bowl which should be heated in a medium oven (mark 4/350 °F). Then place the macaroni in a saucepan of briskly boiling water to which salt and a few drops of oil have been added. Cook it without a lid, according to the instructions on the packet (about 12 minutes). While that's happening, melt a little oil in a frying pan and cook the bacon—not crisply, just until the fat starts to run. Also break the eggs into a bowl, season them with salt and pepper, add the Parmesan and beat with a fork. Now put two plates in the oven to warm, then drain the cooked macaroni in a colander, whip the hot bowl out of the oven and tip the macaroni into it. Quickly add the bacon, followed by the beaten eggs—and stir it all around speedily and deftly. Continue stirring and the eggs will soon cook and turn slightly granular from the heat of the bowl. Serve on to warmed plates with a knob of butter on each serving, and have some grated Parmesan cheese on the table to sprinkle over.

Spaghetti with Olives and Anchovies

(Serves 2)

8 oz spaghetti
1 teaspoon oil
3 tablespoons more oil
8 oz fresh mushrooms, thinly sliced
2 onions, peeled and thinly sliced
2 cloves garlic, crushed
5 anchovy fillets, snipped in half
3 rashers lean bacon, rinded and roughly chopped
6 Spanish stuffed olives, sliced
2 tablespoons chopped parsley
2 tablespoons grated Parmesan cheese
Salt

First of all, heat the 3 tablespoons of oil in a thick-based pan and start to cook the mushrooms, onion, garlic, anchovy fillets and bacon gently. Stir them all around from time to time. Boil the spaghetti in salted water with 1 teaspoon of oil in it for 10 minutes. Then add the parsley and olives to the other ingredients in the pan and heat them through. Now drain the spaghetti in a warmed colander, pile it on to a warmed serving dish and top with the savoury mixture, sprinkled finally with some grated Parmesan cheese.

Macaroni au Gratin

(Serves 3)

4 oz any supermarket macaroni
1½ pints water
1 teaspoon salt
6 oz grated cheese (Cheddar)
2 oz butter
1 level teaspoon dried mustard
1½ oz plain flour
¾ pint milk
4 rashers streaky bacon, rinded and chopped
2 oz mushrooms, sliced
1 medium onion, peeled and chopped
1 tomato, cut into small pieces
A little extra butter
Salt and freshly milled black pepper
A little freshly grated nutmeg

Bring the salted water to the boil in a large pan, add the
macaroni and boil without a lid, according to the instructions
on the packet. Meanwhile melt 2 oz of butter in a saucepan,
add the flour and mustard, and make up a white sauce with
the milk, cooking for about 6 minutes before adding 3 oz of
the grated cheese to melt gently into it, together with a seasoning of salt and pepper and a few gratings of nutmeg. Then in a
little butter in a small frying pan, soften the onion, bacon and
mushroom together for about 6 minutes. Now drain the
macaroni in a colander, combine it with the sauce and the
bacon, onion and mushroom, then place the whole mixture in
a buttered 2-pint baking dish. Sprinkle the rest of the cheese
on top, plus the pieces of tomato. Finish off by placing the
dish under a hot grill until golden brown and bubbling.

Note: If you want to make this in advance, you can re-heat it
in a high oven, mark 6/400 °F, for about 15–20 minutes.

I do, for one. I could never be an out-and-out vegetarian, although I must admit the thought does cross my mind from time to time. But then all I have to do is conjure up a picture of a steaming steak and kidney pud bursting at the seams with fragrant juices or imagine the sound and smell of bacon and eggs sizzling, and I'm instantly cured.

On the other hand, I also think our national pre-occupation with excessive meat-eating is to some extent the result of habit. Once the habit is broken one can live quite happily for days with little or no meat, and I very often do. True, a main meal that doesn't contain any meat (or pulses, which we'll come to later) needs a little more care, needs to be, if you like, a little more special. The scope, however, is enormous: there are literally hundreds of variations on the quiche—just think what a treat a soufflé is, and if you've never tried your hand at a pizza I insist you try it now.

As for faint-hearted wives who complain that their husbands only want meat—well, I've never been liberated or concerned with women's rights, but I do think that if you're going to go to the trouble of cooking for someone the least they can do is eat what you cook. So be firm: send him off to buy his own steak and chops *and* pay for them. If not, blame it all on this book.

Pizza Dough

8 oz plain flour
1 level teaspoon salt
¼ teaspoon sugar
1½ teaspoons dried yeast
1 standard egg, beaten
3–4 fl. oz water (hand-hot)
1 teaspoon oil

First pour 3 fl. oz of hand-hot water into a basin and whisk in the sugar, followed by the yeast; then leave this mixture on one side for about 10–15 minutes until it gets a nice frothy head on it. Meanwhile sift the flour and salt together in a mixing bowl. Then pour in the frothy yeast mixture and the beaten egg, and mix to a dough (you may need to add just a spot of extra warm water—it depends on the flour—but at the end you should have a soft, pliable dough that leaves the bowl clean). Then transfer the dough to a working surface and knead for about 10 minutes until it's silky smooth and fairly elastic.

Now replace the dough in the bowl and rub the surface all over with the oil. Then seal the top of the bowl with cling film—or cover with a clean cloth—and put the dough in a warmish place to rise for about an hour, or until it has doubled in size.

Once the dough has 'proved' (that is, doubled in size), knead it again for about 5 minutes, and then it's ready to use. (All this does in fact *sound* a lot more trouble than it actually is.)

There are many different fillings for pizzas, but here are two combinations that I particularly like. Of course, you can adapt them, if you feel like it, and make up your own variations.

Pizza with Cream Cheese, Olives and Anchovies

(Serves 2–4)

For the tomato sauce:
2 tablespoons oil
1 Spanish onion, peeled and chopped
2 cloves garlic, crushed
2 14-oz tins of Italian tomatoes
¾ teaspoon dried basil (or fresh if you have it)
1 large bayleaf
Salt and freshly milled black pepper

For the garnish:
4 oz cream cheese, cut in small pieces
A 2-oz can anchovy fillets, drained and chopped
1 dozen black olives, pitted and halved
1 teaspoon dried oregano
1 tablespoon grated Parmesan
Oil

Make the pizza dough as described on p. 169.

To prepare the sauce, heat the oil and fry the onion until softened and golden; then stir in the remaining sauce ingredients and simmer gently (uncovered) for about an hour, or until the tomatoes have reduced to a jam-like consistency. Then take the pan off the heat, discard the bayleaf and leave the sauce to cool.

Now select a large dry baking sheet (don't oil it) and push the dough out with your hands to a rectangle roughly 10 × 11 inches—or a round if you prefer. If the dough is very springy, be determined with it. Now pinch up the edges all round to make a sort of border to contain the filling. Then brush the base of the dough with oil, cover with the tomato filling and spread it right up to the pinched edge. Next sprinkle the surface with the cheese, anchovies, halved olives, dried oregano and Parmesan, drizzle about a tablespoon of oil over the top and leave the pizza at room temperature for 10 or 15 minutes before baking. Meanwhile pre-heat the oven to mark 7/425 °F.

Then bake the pizza for 15–20 minutes. Check that the bread base is cooked through in the centre by lifting the pizza up with a fish slice and taking a look. And remember it's better to slightly over-cook than under-cook a pizza, and always serve it fresh straight from the oven if possible.

Pizza with Salami and Mushrooms (Serves 2–4)

A 8-oz tin Italian tomatoes
1 tablespoon tomato purée
1 teaspoon dried basil
6 oz salami or Italian pepperoni sausage
1 tablespoon capers
1 small pepper, de-seeded and finely chopped
2 oz mushrooms, thinly sliced
2 tablespoons grated Parmesan
Oil
Salt and freshly milled black pepper

Pre-heat the oven to mark 7/425°F

Prepare the pizza dough as described on p. 169. Then choose a large baking sheet again, and push the dough out to a rectangle as in the previous recipe. Pinch out a narrow border and brush the base with oil. Now either liquidise the contents of the tin of tomatoes or simply rub them through a sieve into a bowl. Then stir in the tomato purée and basil, taste, and season with salt and freshly milled pepper. Now pour the mixture on to the pizza base and spread it all over. Next skin and thinly slice the salami, and halve the slices. Then arrange them over the top of the pizza, sprinkle on the chopped pepper, capers, sliced mushrooms and grated Parmesan, and again trickle a little oil over the top. Leave the pizza on one side for about 10 minutes before baking in the oven for 15–20 minutes.

Cheese and Vegetable Wholewheat Flan

(Serves 4)

For this recipe (ideal for vegetarians) I use a 7-inch metal pie plate with a rim which is about 1½ inches deep.

For the pastry:
1½ oz wholewheat flour
1½ oz plain flour
1½ oz butter
A pinch salt
Some water

For the filling:
1 carrot, scraped and thinly sliced
3 oz swede, peeled and thinly sliced
3 oz turnip, peeled and thinly sliced
1 stick celery, sliced
1 small onion, peeled and finely chopped
1 small leek, trimmed, washed and finely chopped
2 oz butter
2 oz grated Cheddar cheese
1 dessertspoon finely chopped parsley
2 pinches cayenne pepper
2 large eggs
8 fl. oz milk
Salt and freshly milled black pepper

Pre-heat the oven to mark 4/300 °F

First make the pastry and roll it out to line the tin. Then prick the pastry base and pre-cook it on a baking sheet for 15 minutes. While that's happening, melt the butter in a frying pan and soften all the vegetables in it for 10–15 minutes. Now remove the flan tin from the oven and, using a draining spoon, transfer the vegetables from the pan to the pastry case, season well and sprinkle the grated cheese on top. Next beat the eggs together with the milk, pour the mixture over the vegetables, then sprinkle with parsley and a couple of pinches of cayenne. Return it to the oven (at the same temperature) and bake for about 40 minutes until golden and puffy.

I like this served with some nice nutty brown rice cooked with onion and herbs (see p. 157).

Courgette Soufflé   (Serves 4)

This will make a very impressive lunchtime dish for 4 people.

4 oz courgettes, thinly sliced
4 oz butter
2 tablespoons finely chopped parsley
2 teaspoons finely chopped chives
3 tablespoons flour
$\frac{1}{2}$ pint milk
5 egg yolks
2 oz grated cheese
1 oz grated Parmesan cheese
6 egg whites
Salt and freshly milled black pepper
Freshly grated nutmeg
A little extra butter

Pre-heat the oven to mark 6/400 °F

For this you'll need a $2\frac{1}{2}$-pint soufflé dish, buttered quite generously. Start by cooking the courgettes gently in 2 oz of the butter. Cook them until softened and beginning to colour slightly, then remove them from the heat, season them with salt and pepper, and leave them to cool. Now melt the remaining 2 oz of butter in a saucepan, stir in the flour and cook for a minute or two before gradually adding the milk, stirring all the time. Bring the mixture up to a simmer, still stirring, and let it cook for about 2 or 3 minutes. Take the sauce off the heat now and cool it by sitting the base of the pan in some cold water. As soon as it's cool enough, gradually beat in the egg yolks, followed by the cheeses, parsley and chives. Season with salt, pepper and freshly grated nutmeg. Now beat up the egg whites to the stiff peak stage and carefully fold them into the cheese mixture, using a metal spoon. Next spoon half the soufflé mixture into the prepared dish, sprinkle in the courgette slices and pour the remaining soufflé mixture on top of them. Now place the soufflé dish in a roasting tin, pour a little boiling water in the tin (to a depth of 1 inch) and transfer the whole lot to the oven. Lower the heat to mark 3/325 °F, bake for 40 minutes and then increase the heat to mark 6/400 °F for a further 10 minutes.

Spinach Cream Flan   (Serves 6 as a main course)

If you can't get fresh spinach for this, use 1 lb of frozen, well thawed and drained.

A quantity shortcrust pastry (made with 6 oz flour and 3 oz fat—see p. 40)

For the filling:
2 lb fresh spinach
1 oz butter
½ lb cream cheese
3 eggs
¼ pint milk
Freshly grated nutmeg
2 tablespoons grated Parmesan or any mild cheese
Salt and freshly milled black pepper
A squeeze of lemon juice

Pre-heat the oven to mark 4/350 °F with a baking sheet in it

Start by making the pasty, and line a 10-inch flan tin with it. Prick the pasty base, place the flan tin on the pre-heated baking sheet and bake it for 15 minutes. Then take it out of the oven, leave it on one side to cool and increase the oven heat to mark 5/375 °F. Now prepare the filling by washing the spinach and discarding any coarse stalks or damaged leaves. Wash the leaves thoroughly, drain and place them in a large heavy-based saucepan with the butter and some salt and freshly ground black pepper. (No need to add any water.) Cover the pan and cook the spinach for about 7 minutes, shaking the pan occasionally, until the spinach collapses down into the butter.

Then drain the spinach in a colander very thoroughly, pressing out any excess moisture, and chop it up with a sharp knife. Now place the cream cheese in a bowl and beat in the milk a little at a time, followed by the beaten eggs, Parmesan cheese and a seasoning of salt, pepper and a little grated nutmeg. Now stir the spinach into the cream mixture. Add a squeeze of lemon juice and, if necessary, a bit more seasoning. Then pour the mixture into the flan case and place the flan back on the heated baking sheet. Bake in the top half of the oven for about 40 minutes, or until the filling is nice and puffy and golden on the top.

Soured Cream and Onion Tart
(Serves 4 as a main course)

A quantity shortcrust pastry (made with 6 oz flour and 3 oz fat)

For the filling:
2 lb onions, peeled and very thinly sliced
2 oz butter
1 clove garlic, crushed
¼ teaspoon dried sage
A 5-fl. oz carton soured cream
2–3 tablespoons single cream or top of the milk
Salt and freshly milled black pepper
1 large egg

Pre-heat the oven to mark 4/350 °F

First make the pastry as described on p. 40, line a 10-inch flan tin with it, prick the base and bake it blind in the oven for 15 minutes. Then remove it from the oven and turn the heat up to mark 5/375 °F and place a baking sheet in the oven.

Gently heat the butter in a large saucepan, and put the sliced onions, garlic and sage in the pan. Cover and cook over a low heat for about 15 minutes, shaking the pan occasionally. Then take the lid off and continue to cook (still shaking from time to time) for a further 15–20 minutes, or until the onions form a soft golden mass. Then remove from the heat. Now beat together the creams and egg, and stir this into the onions. Taste and season with salt and pepper. Spread the mixture in the pastry case. Then place the flan on the heated baking sheet in the top half of the oven and bake for about 40 minutes, or until the surface of the tart is lightly browned.

Leek, Carrot and Potato Pie (Serves 3)

This is a complete supper dish made from root vegetables— just the thing if you don't want a heavy meal.

½ lb carrots, scraped and left whole
1 lb potatoes, peeled and left whole
Butter
1 lb leeks, halved lengthways and cut into ¼-inch thick slices
1 small onion, peeled and chopped
½ pint white sauce (made with 1½ oz butter, ¾ oz flour,
   ¼ pint milk, ¼ pint vegetable stock, a pinch ground mace)
Salt and freshly milled black pepper

For the topping:
3 oz grated Cheddar cheese
1 tablespoon breadcrumbs
2 pinches cayenne pepper

Pre-heat the oven to mark 4/350 °F

Bring a saucepan of salted water up to boiling point, then put in the whole potatoes and carrots; bring them to the boil, cover and cook for about 15 minutes. Then drain them, reserving the water. Now return the pan you cooked them in to the heat and melt 2 oz of butter in it. Add the washed, drained leeks and the chopped onion, and cook them gently for about 6 or 7 minutes, or until softened. Now slice the potatoes and carrots thinly and arrange them in layers in a well-buttered baking dish. Then make up the sauce and pour it over the vegetables, scatter the cheese and breadcrumbs and a couple of pinches of cayenne on the top, dot the surface with small flecks of butter and bake for about 1 hour.

Curried Eggs with Cauliflower   (Serves 3)

If you've got a few spices handy, this dish can be made fairly quickly with just a few eggs and a cauliflower, and it tastes quite delicious.

6 eggs
1 large cauliflower
1 tablespoon flour
1 oz butter
1 tablespoon oil
1 onion, peeled and finely chopped
2 teaspoons ground coriander
1 teaspoon tumeric
1 clove garlic, crushed
$\frac{1}{4}$–$\frac{1}{2}$ teaspoon chilli powder (how much depends on you)
$\frac{1}{2}$ pint stock (from the cauliflower water)
2–3 teaspoons mango chutney
A squeeze of lemon juice
2 tablespoons natural yoghurt
Salt

Begin by dividing the cauliflower into small florets. Have ready some boiling, salted water and cook them in it for about 5 minutes. Then drain them and reserve the water. Next heat the butter and oil in a large cooking pot and gently fry the onion until soft; stir in the garlic, spices and flour, and cook for a minute or two before gradually stirring in $\frac{1}{2}$ pint of the cauliflower water. Now bring up to the boil, cover and simmer very gently for 10 minutes. Then stir in the chutney, lemon juice, yoghurt and cauliflower, and cook for a further 5 minutes, tasting to check the seasoning. At some time while all this is happening, carefully lower the eggs into a pan of gently simmering water, simmer for 7 minutes, then cool them under running water. Peel off the shells, halve the eggs and arrange them on a warmed serving dish. Pour the sauce and cauliflower over the top. Serve with rice and mango chutney.

Pancakes with Spinach and Cheese

(Serves 2 or 3)

For a complete meal all this needs is a lot of crusty bread and butter and some fresh fruit to follow.

6 thin pancakes (see p. 220)
1½ lb fresh spinach
3 tablespoons butter
4–5 tablespoons double cream
Salt and freshly milled black pepper
¾ pint cheese sauce (made with 2 oz butter, 1½ oz flour,
   ¾ pint milk and 3 oz grated cheese)
1 oz grated Parmesan
Freshly grated nutmeg
A little extra butter

Pre-heat the oven to mark 6/400°F

First prepare the spinach by washing it in several changes of water. Discard any damaged leaves and pick out any thick stalks. Press the leaves firmly into a large saucepan and sprinkle with about a teaspoon of salt. Don't add any water, just cover the pan and cook over a fairly high heat for about 7 or 8 minutes. While it cooks, remove the lid once or twice and churn the spinach around a bit with a wooden spoon. Then drain the spinach in a colander, pressing out as much excess liquid as possible. Now chop the spinach, melt the butter in a frying pan and add the chopped spinach to the pan, followed by the cream. Stir (a wooden fork is good here to break up the spinach) and cook until there is no excess cream and you have a nice moist mixture to fill the pancakes. Taste and season with salt and freshly milled pepper, and a good grating of whole nutmeg. Now arrange an equal quantity of the spinach mixture on each pancake and roll them up; then place them in a well-buttered gratin dish and pour over the prepared sauce. Finally sprinkle the surface with the grated cheese and bake near the top of the oven for 25 minutes, until it's nicely browned and bubbling.

Baked Marrow with Sage and Cheese

(Serves 4)

This is an excellent meatless supper dish, especially when marrows are very cheap around the latter half of August.

A 3¼-lb marrow
4 oz Wensleydale cheese, grated
¾ teaspoon dried sage
1 medium onion, peeled and thinly sliced
3 tablespoons dry white breadcrumbs
Salt and freshly milled black pepper

Pre-heat the oven to mark 2/300°F

Trim off both ends of the marrow and peel it, using a potato peeler if you've got one; then halve the marrow lengthways and scoop out and discard all the fibre and seeds. Now cut it into ¼-inch thick slices and then halve the slices. Put a third of the marrow in a layer in the base of a 4-pint casserole. Sprinkle with a third of the grated cheese, ¼ teaspoon of sage, half the sliced onion and a little salt and pepper. Repeat this layering once more, then finish off with a layer of marrow and some seasoning. Next mix the remaining cheese with the breadcrumbs and sprinkle all over the top. Cover loosely with a sheet of foil and bake for 1 hour. Then uncover and bake for a further hour, or until the vegetables are tender when tested with a skewer. Serve hot—or it's even nicer served cold if the weather's very hot.

QUICKENING PULSES

There was a startling report by the Consumers' Association earlier this year which stated that anyone in this country could survive (foodwise) on £2 per week! What's more they told us how, and one of the top-rated foods for protein and value were the various pulses (or legumes as they're sometimes called); lentils, dried peas, beans, etc.

It wasn't so long ago that these raw materials were overlooked by all except vegetarians. Nowadays, not only are they highly regarded as important sources of protein but also the path-finders of commercialism have begun to use these vegetable proteins to make imitation meat. Never mind if meat is short, they say, we'll just *pretend* we've got it. So Britain was presented with her first samples of TVP (textured vegetable protein), and the Press with a host of funny 'can-you-tell-the-difference' stories.

Nutritionists (often indirectly on the payrolls of the companies producing TVP) said we were all going to *have* to eat it for future survival. Happily, it hasn't yet caught on (not that producers are deterred—it took 100 years for margarine to be universally accepted). In spite of all the nice people who have tried hard to convince me, the facts as I see them are these:

(*a*) If we can't have meat in the future, then let's not pretend we can—let's evolve in a more realistic direction.

(*b*) Vegetable proteins (as in this chapter) can be cooked and eaten as they are without the expense of refining and disguising them.

(*c*) The promoters of TVP point out that it's not meant to be eaten on its own, it's meant to extend meat. As a cook I'm bound to say there are far pleasanter ways of eking out meat if it's simply for bulk; ordinary vegetables, onion, carrot, celery, turnip, swede, all add flavours of their own. And if it's to increase protein, then why not add our pulses as they are, with their own flavour and texture? It might not be so convenient in the school canteen, but at least our children would be pointed in the right direction for the future instead of being deceived by pretend meat.

And now I'm off my soap-box, one positive aspect of the situation is that farmers are at last experimenting with lentil production in this country, and I'm told that soya production may well yield over a ton an acre within five years. I hope they succeed.

Chilladas

These little lentil rissoles are, in my opinion, even better than those made with meat, and they're delicious served with the Tomato Chilli Sauce on p. 145.

8 oz green or brown whole lentils
¾ pint hot water
2 oz butter or vegetable margarine
1 medium onion, peeled and finely chopped
1 small green pepper, de-seeded and chopped small
1 medium carrot, scraped and finely chopped
½ teaspoon mixed herbs
¼ teaspoon powdered mace
½ teaspoon cayenne pepper
2 teaspoons tomato purée
1 clove garlic, crushed
Salt and freshly milled black pepper

Then to coat them:
Dry fine breadcrumbs
1 egg, beaten
Enough groundnut oil for shallow frying

Wash and pick over the lentils, then place them in a saucepan with ¾ pint hot water and some salt. When they come to the boil, cover and simmer very gently for about an hour, or until all the liquid has been absorbed and the lentils are mushy. Towards the end of their cooking time, heat the butter or magarine in a frying pan and soften the onion, garlic and carrot in it for 5 minutes; then add the chopped pepper and cook for a further 5 or 10 minutes. Next tip the cooked lentils into a bowl and mash them to a pulp with a fork (not too uniformly smooth). Now mix in the softened vegetables, cayenne, mace, herbs and tomato purée, then divide the mixture and shape into 12 small rounds. All this can be done in advance. To cook them, dip them first in beaten egg, then in breadcrumbs. Shallow fry them in about ¼ inch of groundnut oil till golden on both sides, then drain on kitchen paper and serve with the sauce.

Chick Pea Salad

(Serves 4–6)

½ lb chick peas (soaked overnight)
8 oz haricots verts (green string beans)
¼ pint garlic-flavoured mayonnaise
A 2-oz tin anchovy fillets, finely chopped
6 spring onions, finely chopped
2 tablespoons capers, chopped
2 tablespoons finely chopped parsley
Lemon juice to taste
A dozen pitted black olives halved
A few crisp lettuce leaves
Salt and freshly milled black pepper

Bring the chick peas to the boil and simmer until tender (about 30 to 45 minutes). Don't salt the water, though, or the chick peas will soften. The topped and tailed haricots will need 3 or 4 minutes in boiling salted water, then drain them with cold water and cut each bean in half. Combine the mayonnaise, anchovy fillets, spring onions, capers, chopped parsley, and add salt and pepper. Then fold the drained chick peas and green beans into the mayonnaise mixture together with the black olives. Taste and add a little lemon juice and more seasoning if necessary. Serve on a bed of crisp lettuce leaves.

Boston Baked Beans

(Serves 4)

This is how Baked Beans should be, the real American sort, not a bit like the ones that come in tins.

1 lb dried white haricot beans
3 pints water
1 onion, peeled and sliced
2 cloves garlic, crushed
1 bayleaf
1 teaspoon English mustard powder
2 tablespoons black treacle
2 tablespoons dark brown sugar
2 tablespoons tomato purée
¾ lb streaky belly of pork, in one piece
Salt and freshly milled black pepper

Measure 3 pints of water into a large saucepan, add the beans, bring to the boil and boil gently for about 2–3 minutes; then remove the pan from the heat and leave on one side for about 1 hour, or until the water has cooled. Now return the beans to the heat and simmer uncovered until the bean skins burst when you lift them out of the water (which will take around 45 minutes). Drain the beans next, reserving the liquor, then measure the liquor and make it up to 1 pint with water if necessary. Transfer the beans to a casserole and pre-heat the oven to mark 1/250 °F.

At this stage, blend the mustard powder with a little of the measured bean liquor, followed by the black treacle, sugar, tomato purée and crushed garlic, and pour this mixture over the beans along with the measured pint of liquid, some seasoning, the sliced onion and a bayleaf. Now cut slashes across the pork (approximately ½ inch apart) and bury the meat in the beans until only the rind is showing. Then cover the casserole closely and bake very slowly for about 6 hours. During the last hour of cooking, take the lid off the casserole to allow the rind on the pork to crisp a little. Also keep stirring the beans during this last hour and, if it shows signs of getting too dry, add just a spot more water. Serve very hot.

Dhal Curry

(Serves 2)

Dhal is simply the Indian word for lentils. The best kind to use for this are the red split lentils which most supermarkets stock.

8 oz red lentils
1 teaspoon each ground ginger, ground cumin and turmeric
1 teaspoon salt
4 tomatoes, peeled and chopped
2 potatoes, peeled and diced
1 large onion, sliced
1 small green pepper, chopped
2 tablespoons butter
1 level teaspoon Madras curry powder (if you like your curries hotter, you can add more)
1 clove garlic, crushed
1 extra teaspoon ground ginger

In a saucepan containing 1½ pints of water add the ginger, cumin, turmeric and salt, then bring it all to the boil. Stir in the lentils, let it come back to a gentle simmer and cook for 5 minutes. After that add the diced potato and continue cooking until the lentils have turned mushy (making sure the mixture doesn't stick to the bottom of the pan by giving it a stir now and again). While that's cooking, heat up the butter in another pan and fry the onions and pepper in it (over a fairly high heat) until the onions have browned—then lower the heat and stir in the Madras curry powder, the garlic, extra ground ginger and chopped tomatoes. Cook for a minute before adding the lentil mixture, then taste, season with salt and cook gently for a further 5–10 minutes (stirring from time to time). Serve this with rice and yoghurt.

Spiced Chick Pea Cutlets

(Serves 3)

Chick peas, sometimes called garbanzos, are available in wholefood shops; but they do need a long soaking, so try to think ahead.

8 oz chick peas (soaked overnight in plenty of cold water)
2 tablespoons oil
1 onion, peeled and finely chopped
1 small green pepper, de-seeded and finely chopped
1 clove garlic, crushed
2 teaspoons tomato purée
2 tablespoons natural yoghurt
½ teaspoon Madras curry powder
½ teaspoon cayenne pepper
Dry white breadcrumbs (for coating)
Oil for shallow frying
Salt and freshly milled black pepper

First tip the soaked chick peas, and their water, into a saucepan. Bring them up to the boil, cover and simmer for about 30 minutes, or until they're absolutely tender. Then drain well, and mash them to a pulp. Now put the 2 tablespoons of oil in a saucepan and gently fry the onion and green pepper until softened; then beat them into the mashed chick peas together with all the remaining ingredients (except, of course, the breadcrumbs and frying oil). Do a bit of tasting at this stage, and season with some salt and pepper. As soon as it's cool enough to handle, form the mixture into 6 patties and coat each one with breadcrumbs. Put about 2 tablespoons of oil in a frying pan and fry the patties to a golden brown colour. Serve them hot garnished with slices of raw Spanish onion and some natural yoghurt as a sauce.

White Bean and Salami Salad   (Serves 4)

This is a delicious salad to serve at lunchtime at any time of the year but especially in the summer. Make sure you have plenty of crusty bread to go with it to mop up the juices.

1 lb dried large haricot beans
1 onion, peeled and stuck with 6 cloves
A few parsley stalks
1 bayleaf
1 clove garlic, crushed
½ teaspoon dried thyme or a sprig of fresh
Salt and freshly milled black pepper

For the dressing:
¼ pint oil—olive or groundnut
2 tablespoons wine vinegar
2 tablespoons dry cider
1 teaspoon mustard powder
1 clove garlic, crushed
1 teaspoon salt
Freshly milled black pepper

Then:
4 oz salami, chopped small
1 medium onion, peeled and thinly sliced
1 tablespoon chopped fresh parsley

First put the dried beans in a sieve and wash them under cold running water. Then place them in a saucepan, add enough cold water to come up about 2 inches above the beans and bring to the boil. As soon as the water boils, switch off the heat and leave the beans to soak for about an hour. Then add the onion stuck with cloves, the parsley, bayleaf, garlic and thyme. Bring the beans back to the boil and simmer very gently without a lid for 1–1½ hours, or until the beans are tender. The length of cooking time really depends on the age of the beans. While the beans are cooking you can make the dressing by dissolving the salt in the wine vinegar for about half an hour and then adding all the other ingredients. To blend them, shake them in a screw-topped jar, then taste and add more pepper and salt if you think it needs it because this dressing needs to be very well seasoned. When the beans are cooked, drain them, and whilst they are still warm combine them with the dressing in a large mixing bowl. Mix them gently to avoid the beans breaking, then add the onion, salami and parsley, and leave for at least an hour before serving.

Lentil, Bean and Anchovy Salad
(Serves 4)

This makes a very inexpensive lunch dish for 4 people along with some crusty bread to mop up the juices.

8 oz whole lentils (brown)
8 oz white haricot beans
Salt and freshly milled black pepper

For the dressing:
8 tablespoons oil
1 tablespoon wine vinegar
1 tablespoon lemon juice
1 small onion, peeled and finely chopped
1 heaped teaspoon mustard
1 clove garlic, crushed
4 tablespoons finely chopped fresh parsley
A 2-oz can anchovy fillets

To garnish:
2 hardboiled eggs, chopped
1 oz small black olives
A few crisp lettuce leaves

In advance you'll need to put the beans in a saucepan with plenty of cold water to cover, then bring to the boil, boil for 2–3 minutes and remove them from the heat. Leave them for about an hour to soak, then boil them again until *just* soft, probably another hour. There's no need to soak the lentils: just pick over them, wash them and boil them in plenty of water until again *just* soft (about 25 minutes). Meanwhile make up the dressing by mixing everything together in a bowl and adding the oil from the tin of anchovies as well. (Chop the anchovies and keep them on one side.) As soon as the beans and lentils are cooked, drain them, and while they're still warm pour on the dressing, toss them around in it and leave to cool. Then taste and season the mixture well with salt and freshly milled pepper. To serve, place some of the bean-and-lentil mixture on to crisp lettuce leaves divided between 4 plates and garnish with the chopped hardboiled eggs, chopped anchovies and olives.

Curried Egg and Lentil Patties (Serves 3)

¼ lb green or brown whole lentils
3 standard eggs, hardboiled and chopped
12 fl. oz water
1 largish onion, peeled and finely chopped
1 clove garlic, crushed
1 tablespoon chopped fresh parsley
⅛–¼ teaspoon chilli powder
¼ teaspoon ground cumin
¼ teaspoon ground coriander
¼ teaspoon ground ginger
¼ teaspoon turmeric
2 oz butter or margarine
Salt and freshly milled black pepper
Groundnut oil for frying
1 egg, beaten and wholemeal flour

Cook the lentils till mushy, as in the previous recipe, then soften the onion and garlic in the butter, add them to the lentils with the chopped eggs, spices, parsley, salt and pepper, and mix thoroughly. When cool, shape the mixture into 9 little patties. Dip them first in beaten egg, then in wholemeal flour and shallow fry them till golden on both sides. Drain on kitchen paper and serve on a bed of spiced pilau rice (see p. 157), garnished with slices of raw onion, and eat with mango chutney and a dollop of natural yoghurt.

Lentil and Split Pea Loaf   (Serves 4)

This is nice served with tomato sauce or some yoghurt and is equally good eaten cold with salad or taken on a picnic in the summer.

6 oz green or brown lentils
4 oz split peas (yellow or green), picked over and rinsed
1 pint vegetable stock or water
1 medium onion, peeled and chopped
½ green pepper, de-seeded and chopped
2 carrots, scraped and chopped
2 sticks celery, chopped
1 fat clove garlic, crushed
1 egg
¼ teaspoon thyme
¼ teaspoon marjoram
2 tablespoons chopped parsley
Salt and freshly milled black pepper

Pre-heat the oven to mark 5/375 °F

First bring the stock or water up to boiling point, then stir in the split peas and simmer (with a lid on) for about 5 minutes. Next add the lentils and herbs and simmer, covered, for a further 25–30 minutes, or until all the liquid has been absorbed and the lentils and peas are soft; then remove the pan from the heat. Now, in another pan, heat the butter and fry all the prepared vegetables and garlic until golden—about 10 minutes. Then stir the mixture into the lentils with the beaten egg and parsley. Taste and season with salt and freshly milled pepper. Spoon the mixture into a well-greased 1-lb loaf tin, cover with foil and bake for 40 minutes. When it's cooked, slip a knife around the inside edge and turn out on to a warmed serving plate.

Haricot and Lentil Chilli   (Serves 4)

Whether you're a vegetarian or not, some meals without meat will eventually become a necessity—but that does not mean they can't be just as good, as this proves.

4 oz haricot beans
4 oz whole brown or green lentils
2 oz pearl barley
2 oz butter
1 large onion, peeled and chopped
2 cloves garlic, crushed
3 carrots, scraped and thinly sliced
4 sticks celery, sliced across thinly
A 14-oz tin Italian tomatoes
1 tablespoon tomato purée
$\frac{1}{4}$–$\frac{1}{2}$ teaspoon chilli powder
1 green pepper, de-seeded and chopped
1 bayleaf
Salt and freshly milled black pepper

First of all put the haricot beans in a small saucepan with
plenty of cold water to cover, then bring them to the boil and
boil gently for 2 or 3 minutes. Remove them from the heat,
cover and leave on one side to soak for about an hour. After
that bring them to the boil again, cover and simmer for 30
minutes; then strain the beans, reserving all their liquor.
While all this is happening, you can very carefully pick over
the lentils, then put them in a sieve with the pearl barley and
rinse thoroughly under the cold water tap. Transfer them to a
bowl, pour some boiling water over them to cover and leave
them to soak for half an hour; then drain them, this time
discarding the water. Now heat the butter until frothy in a
casserole and gently soften the onion, garlic, carrot and
celery (but don't brown them). Then add the tomatoes and
purée, and stir in the drained lentils and barley, and the
drained beans and their reserved cooking liquor (made up to
$\frac{1}{2}$ pint with fresh water). Now sprinkle in the chilli powder,
add the bayleaf, bring to simmering point, cover and continue
to simmer for half an hour. Then add the chopped pepper
and continue to simmer for a further 30 minutes, or until
everything is just tender. Taste and season with salt and
pepper. Add a little more water if you feel it's needed. Re-heat
and serve with some nutty brown rice cooked with onion.

Lentil and Vegetable Curry (Serves 6)

½ lb runner beans, stringed and sliced
½ lb potatoes, peeled and diced into ½-inch pieces
½ lb cauliflower, separated into small florets
2 medium carrots, scraped and sliced
4 tablespoons oil
1 large onion, peeled and chopped
2 teaspoons turmeric powder
½ teaspoon ground coriander
2 teaspoons cumin seeds
2 teaspoons finely chopped fresh ginger (or 1 teaspoon ground)
1 fat clove garlic, crushed
12 oz brown lentils (picked over and rinsed)
½ pint natural yoghurt
1 rounded tablespoon tomato purée
Salt
½–¾ teaspoon cayenne pepper

Blanch the beans, potatoes, carrots and cauliflower by placing them in a pan containing 1¾ pints of boiling salted water. Cover and cook gently for 6 minutes; then drain, reserving the water. Now heat the oil in a pan and fry the onion until softened. Then stir in the turmeric, coriander, cumin seeds, ginger and garlic, followed by the lentils, and stir until everything is thoroughly combined before pouring in the reserved vegetable water. Now bring to the boil, cover and cook gently for 40 minutes, or until the lentils are just tender. Next add the blanched vegetables to the lentil mixture along with the yoghurt, tomato purée and just ½ teaspoon of cayenne pepper. Stir well, and try to push all the vegetables below the surface of the liquid. Now bring to simmering point, cover and cook for a further 20 minutes, or until everything is tender. Taste and add a further ¼ teaspoon of cayenne, if you prefer a hotter flavour, and season with salt. Serve with rice.

BACK TO BAKING

As I see it, there are two important reasons for home baking. One is that as often as not 50 per cent of the shop price can be saved; the other is that it's almost always bound to taste better. As ever, time is the enemy, but quite honestly how much time does it really take to make a few biscuits, a cake and perhaps a few scones? Grandma's 'baking-day' principle still holds good —perhaps more so now that fuel prices have risen. Once the oven is on, it's best to make full use of it and pop in a batch of baking (provided you have a few airtight tins to keep your biscuits, cakes, etc. in).

I find home baking particularly self-satisfying and a great incentive to revive that neglected meal, the British Tea, especially at weekends. As for baking bread, if you've never made bread in your life I guarantee you'll find it a whole lot easier than it sounds (not to say cheaper, and so delicious that everyone will eat far too much of it and not be able to manage anything else!).

Strawberry Jam Sponge

I've always found the classic Victoria Sponge very dull and, frankly, not worth the trouble. Then along came soft margarine, and now it takes 2 minutes to whip up a sponge that's light, moist and keeps perfectly fresh in an airtight tin.

4 oz self-raising flour
1 level teaspoon baking powder
4 oz soft margarine at room temperature (I use Blue Band)
4 oz caster sugar
2 large eggs
2–3 drops vanilla essence

Pre-heat the oven to mark 3/325 °F

For this you will need two 7-inch sponge tins, lightly buttered and their bases lined with greaseproof paper (these tins should be no less than 1 inch deep—Tower make them in their non-stick range). The size of the tins in cake making is absolutely vital—and no other sizes will do.

Combine all the ingredients in a mixing bowl and whisk with an electric hand-whisk for about 2 minutes, or until everything is thoroughly mixed. Now divide the mixture between the two prepared tins, level off and bake on the centre shelf of the oven for about 30 minutes. When cooked, leave them in the tins for only about 30 seconds before turning them out on to a wire cooling tray. When cool, sandwich together with strawberry jam, dust the top with sifted icing sugar and store in an airtight tin.

Sticky Tea Bread

This is unbelievably simple to make—it's dark and sticky and gets much better with a few days' keeping.

¼ pint water
4 oz sultanas
5 oz caster sugar
¼ lb butter
1 teaspoon bicarbonate of soda
6 oz plain flour
1 egg
1 teaspoon baking powder

Pre-heat the oven to mark 4/350 °F

First grease a 1-lb loaf tin and line it with greaseproof paper, also greased. Then take a large thick-based saucepan and put into it the water, sugar, sultanas, butter and bicarbonate of soda. Place the pan on a medium heat, stir the ingredients together and bring them up to the boil. Then boil for 10 minutes exactly—but don't go away, watch it like a hawk, because if the temperature isn't controlled it might boil over. When the 10 minutes is up, remove the pan from the heat and allow the mixture to cool. Then add the beaten egg, and the baking powder and flour sifted. Give it a good mix, then place the mixture in the prepared tin and bake it for about 1½ hours on the middle shelf.

Irish Soda Bread

This is a good, easy, standby recipe for days when you suddenly need extra bread and you have no yeast available. It isn't a 'keeping' loaf, though, and is best eaten fresh.

8 oz wholemeal flour
8 oz plain flour
1 level teaspoon salt
1 teaspoon bicarbonate of soda
2 teaspoons cream of tartar
1 teaspoon sugar
2 oz butter
½ pint milk

Pre-heat the oven to mark 5/375 °F

First take a large bowl and sift the flour, salt, bicarbonate of soda, sugar and cream of tartar into it; then rub in the butter, using your fingertips, until it is thoroughly blended. Now mix in the milk, first with a wooden spoon then with your hands, until you have a nice soft dough; then knead it for a minute or two in the bowl, sprinkling in a little more flour if it feels sticky. Transfer the dough on to a lightly floured board and shape it neatly into a round. Now, using the back of a knife, score the top of the dough quite deeply, making a cross, and leave it for 10 minutes. After that, place the loaf on a greased baking sheet and bake it for about 30–40 minutes, or until it sounds hollow when tapped underneath. Then wrap it in a clean teacloth to keep the steam in, allow it to cool and serve it as fresh as possible.

Sugarless Orange and Sultana Cake

This recipe was snipped out of the *Evening Standard* in 1940 by a reader and it was very popular during the 1974 sugar crisis.

3 oz margarine or butter
¼ pint sweetened condensed milk
2 eggs, whisked until frothy
6 oz self-raising flour
4 oz sultanas
Grated rind of 1 orange
1 tablespoon orange juice
Melted lard or butter

Pre-heat the oven to mark 3/325°F

Line the base of a deep, round 7-inch cake tin with a circle of greaseproof paper and brush the tin and paper with melted fat—lard or butter. Now place the butter (or margarine) in a bowl and beat until softened and light. Then gradually beat in the condensed milk, followed by the beaten eggs, a little at a time. Now carefully fold in the sifted flour, sultanas, orange rind and juice. Mix thoroughly and spoon the mixture into the prepared tin. Bake in the centre of the oven for 1 hour, or until the cake shows signs of shrinking away from the side of the tin and is nicely risen and browned. Then turn the cake out on to a wire rack and leave to cool.

Wheatmeal Shortbread

If you're hard up and need to give someone a present, this would be ideal packed in a pretty tin. It is, in fact, a variation on the usual Scotch shortbread, only using brown flour and sugar, and some rice flour to give an extra crisp bite to it.

6 oz wheatmeal flour (85 per cent flour), or 4 oz wholemeal and
  2 oz plain white
2 oz ground rice
¼ teaspoon salt
2 oz caster sugar
5 oz butter (room temperature)
A little extra caster sugar

Pre-heat the oven to mark 3/325°F

Begin by beating the butter in a bowl and gradually working in the flour, ground rice, sugar and salt (using your hands at the end to form the mixture into a stiff dough)—but don't work it too much or the butter will get oily. Then divide the dough in half, and roll out one piece to a 6-inch round. Now transfer the round to a greased baking sheet, pinching all round the edge to decorate. Then, using the back of a knife, mark the round into 8 wedges, and prick all over with a fork. Do the same with the remaining piece of dough, then sprinkle both rounds with a little caster sugar. Now bake just below the centre of the oven for 40–45 minutes, or until both short-breads are tinged brown and feel firm in the centre. Then remove them from the oven, sprinkle again with a little more caster sugar and leave till cooled a little before cutting each round into the marked wedges. Cool them on a wire rack and store in an airtight tin. If you prefer, you can roll the dough out to a ½-inch thick round and cut the shortbread into wedges with a small fluted cutter.

Quick Wholemeal Bread

This recipe is one I have adapted from one given by Doris Grant in her excellent book on wholefoods, *Your Daily Food*. For it you will need a 2-lb loaf tin (well greased and warmed slightly) or two 1-lb loaf tins.

1 lb stoneground wholewheat flour
1 teaspoon salt
12 fl. oz hand hot water (i.e. water that you can hold your finger in for a few moments without burning it)
1 teaspoon dark brown sugar
2 level teaspoons dried yeast

Pre-heat the oven to mark 6/400°F

Carefully measure 1 lb of flour into a mixing bowl (slightly warm the flour first in cold weather), and add the salt. Now pour ¼ pint of the water into a jug, add the dark brown sugar, sprinkle in the dried yeast, then stir well. Then leave it on one side for 10–15 minutes until it displays a good frothy head. When it's ready, pour the yeast liquid into the flour (mixing with a wooden spoon), then add the rest of the water gradually to make a dough that is slightly moister than usual but will eventually leave the bowl clean. Place the dough in the slightly warmed loaf tin(s), even it out, cover with a clean cloth, then leave in a warm place for about 25 minutes—or until the dough has risen to within an inch of the top of the tin. Finally, dust the top with a little wholewheat flour and bake on a high shelf in the oven for 40–45 minutes. To test if it is cooked, take the bread out of the tin and tap the underneath—you should get a hollow sound. Then leave it to cool on a wire tray.

Note: If the dough takes longer to rise than expected, don't worry, just leave it until it *is* within an inch of the top of the tin.

Date, Prune and Walnut Loaf

This is a nice nutty wholemeal cake, delicious cut in thick slices and spread with butter.

3 oz dried prunes, soaked overnight
4 oz butter (room temperature)
6 oz soft brown sugar
2 eggs, lightly beaten
4 oz wholewheat flour
4 oz plain flour
A pinch salt
1 level teaspoon baking powder
4 oz walnuts, roughly chopped
3 oz pitted dates
3 or 4 tablespoons milk

Pre-heat the oven to mark 4/350°F

First well butter a 5 × 9 inch loaf tin. Then after soaking the prunes, drain them thoroughly, take out the stones and chop the flesh into largish pieces. Now in a large mixing bowl cream the butter and sugar together till pale white and fluffy, then add the beaten eggs a little at a time, beating well after each addition. Next sift the flours, salt and baking powder and, using a metal spoon, fold them carefully into the creamed mixture. Now add the prunes, dates and walnuts, followed by the milk, and mix them in before transferring the mixture to the tin. Spread it out evenly, then bake for 1 hour, or until the loaf feels springy in the centre and a skewer inserted in the middle comes out clean. Let the cake cool for a minute or two in the tin, then turn it out on to a wire tray to cool and store in an airtight tin.

Old-fashioned Seed Cake

I think this is best kept in an airtight tin to mature for a couple of days.

4 oz butter
4 oz caster sugar
2 beaten eggs
5 oz self-raising flour
1 oz ground almonds
2–3 tablespoons milk
2 teaspoons caraway seeds
12 sugar cubes, lightly crushed with a rolling pin

Pre-heat the oven to mark 4/350 °F

Start by greasing a 7-inch round cake tin and lining the base with a circle of greaseproof paper cut to fit; then grease the paper too. Cream the butter and sugar together until the mixture is pale and fluffy. Then beat in the eggs a little at a time, and lightly fold in the ground almonds, caraway seeds and flour, followed by enough milk to give the mixture a good dropping consistency. Now spoon the mixture into the prepared tin, level off the surface with the back of a tablespoon and sprinkle with the crushed sugar cubes. Bake the cake in the centre of the oven for about 1 hour, or until the cake feels springy in the centre and shows signs of shrinking away from the side of the tin. Cool on a wire rack.

Oat Crunch Biscuits

Making these delicious little biscuits at home will cost you half what you would pay in the shops. These ingredients are enough for 12 biscuits.

4½ oz porridge oats
4 oz butter (or margarine)
3 oz demerara sugar

Pre-heat the oven to mark 5/375 °F

Well butter a shallow baking tin (11 × 7 inches). Then melt the 4 oz of butter gently in a saucepan, without letting it colour, and mix the sugar and porridge oats evenly in a mixing bowl. Now pour the melted butter into the mixture, and mix until all the ingredients are well and truly blended together. And all you have to do now is press this mixture all over the base of the baking tin and then bake in the oven for 15 minutes, or until they are a nice pale golden colour. Take the tin out of the oven, and cut the mixture into 12 portions – then leave in the tin until quite cold and crisp before removing them to an airtight tin (if you want to store them).

Butterfly Cakes

(To make about 18)

Very simple little cakes these, but it's amazing how quickly they disappear, especially if there are children around.

6 oz self-raising flour
4 oz soft margarine
$\frac{1}{2}$ teaspoon baking powder
4 oz caster sugar
2 eggs, beaten
1 dessertspoon coffee essence (i.e. Camp)
1 dessertspoon milk
A 5-fl. oz carton double cream
Coffee essence to taste
Icing sugar

Pre-heat the oven to mark 5/375°F

Place the flour, baking powder, sugar, soft margarine, eggs, dessertspoon of coffee essence and milk in a large mixing bowl and whisk them together for about 1 minute, or until thoroughly blended. Now arrange 18 paper cake-cases in bun tins. Spoon about 1 heaped teaspoonful of cake mixture into each paper case, putting (as far as possible) an equal quantity of mixture in each case. Then bake in the top half of the oven for about 20 minutes, or until each cake is well risen and has stopped bubbling.

Then remove the cakes to a wire rack to cool and, meanwhile, in a basin whip the cream with about a dessertspoon of coffee essence (or more if you prefer). Scoop a little cone off the top of each cake (a grapefruit knife is good for this), place a heaped teaspoon of cream in each cavity, then cut each little cone in half and arrange like butterfly wings on the top of the cream. Finally give them a light dusting of icing sugar and serve.

PAUPER'S PUDDINGS

One thing I've learned about nutritionists is that they rarely agree with each other. But since one thing they *do* agree about is that sugar (white or brown) is not necessary when people are eating normal balanced diets, I assume there is something in it. Dentists, of course, would ban it completely (except that would probably make a few of them redundant).

I agree that sugar-eating is an addiction and, unfortunately, I'm addicted to a certain extent—and very often what is bad for you medically can be good psychologically (it's amazing how quickly I perk up at the prospect of a Mars bar when I'm down in the dumps).

My real complaint about sugar in recipes, though, is that it can so easily kill flavour. Take chocolate recipes, for instance: if a recipe says plain chocolate, then it shouldn't say sugar as well, because plain chocolate already has sugar in it. So my advice is to slash your calorie intake and your budget simultaneously by gradually cutting down on sugar consumption and by looking carefully at all sweet recipes to determine whether the sugar is essential to the recipe or is there to pander to our addiction.

Honeycomb Mould   (Serves 4)

There are many commercial factory-made versions of this, but homemade it's so much nicer.

1 pint milk
Rind and juice of 2 lemons
3 eggs
3 oz granulated sugar
1½ tablespoons gelatine powder dissolved in 2 tablespoons
   water

First place the milk in a saucepan with the thinly pared rind of the lemons. Bring slowly to the boil while separating the eggs into two basins. Then mix the sugar into the yolks. Strain the milk through a sieve on to the egg yolks and sugar, and whisk well before returning the mixture to the saucepan. Then stand the pan over a medium heat and stir until the liquid has almost reached boiling point and has thickened to a thinnish custard consistency. Now take the pan from the heat and leave it on one side to cool. Next sprinkle the gelatine into a small cup or basin containing 2 tablespoons of water. Leave it for a few minutes to give the gelatine time to soften, then place the cup in an inch of simmering water in a saucepan. Stir occasionally until the gelatine has dissolved and the liquid is absolutely clear. Then strain it into the cooling custard, mix thoroughly and, when the custard is cold, stir in the lemon juice. Now whisk the egg whites until stiff but not dry, and carefully fold them into the custard mixture. Pour the mixture into a 2½-pint basin and leave in a cool place to set—bearing in mind that it will separate into 3 layers: a clear jelly top, a creamy centre and a moussey base. Lovely!

Caramelised Apples

(Serves 4)

1½ lb cooking apples
3 tablespoons water
A vanilla pod
1 tablespoon apricot jam
½ oz butter
Sugar to taste

For the caramel:
3 oz granulated sugar

Peel, core and slice the apples into a saucepan, add 3 table-spoons of water plus the vanilla pod, cover and cook very gently until the apples are soft. Then turn off the heat under the pan and remove the vanilla pod (which can be rinsed, dried and used again). Now add the butter and apricot jam to the pan and, after a minute or two, beat the mixture to a purée. Taste and add a bit more sugar if you think it needs it. Now spread the apple pulp in a heatproof bowl, cover and chill in the refrigerator.

To make the caramel, simply put the sugar in a saucepan and heat until it starts to dissolve around the edge and darken. Shake the pan gently and continue heating, stirring once or twice with a wooden spoon; continue to cook until the syrup formed is a shade darker than golden syrup. Now pour im-mediately over the apples and chill again until firm and cold. Tap the caramel surface all over with a spoon to break it up before serving—and some chilled 'real' custard would be lovely with it.

Rhubarb and Orange Flan   (Serves 6)

The orange in this recipe brings out the flavour of rhubarb beautifully.

For the pastry:
3 oz fine oatmeal
5 oz flour
2 teaspoons soft brown sugar
2 oz lard
2 oz butter

For the filling:
2 lb rhubarb, trimmed, washed and cut into 1-inch chunks
3 oz soft brown sugar
Rind and juice of 1 small orange
1 level tablespoon cornflour

Pre-heat the oven to mark 4/350 °F

First of all place the rhubarb in a casserole, sprinkle it with the sugar, the orange zest and orange juice, and bake it uncovered for around 20–30 minutes, or until tender when tested with a skewer; then take it out of the oven and allow to cool. While it's cooling, make the pastry. Place the dry ingredients in a mixing bowl, rub in the fats to the fine 'breadcrumbs' stage, then add enough water to make a smooth dough. Roll it out and line an 8- or 9-inch flan tin with it (and reserve the pastry trimmings). Now prick the base and bake the flan case for about 25–30 minutes (temperatures as above); then remove it and increase the heat to mark 7/425 °F. Meanwhile drain the rhubarb in a sieve placed over a bowl to reserve the juice, then mix the juice with the cornflour in a small saucepan until smooth, and simmer for 2 minutes. Now arrange the rhubarb in the cooked flan case, pour the sauce over and decorate the top with the pastry trimmings re-rolled and cut into thinnish strips ($\frac{1}{4}$ inch wide) to make a sort of lattice-work pattern over the rhubarb. Now put it back into the oven and let it cook for a further 15 minutes. Serve warm with thick cream.

English Gooseberry Pie

(Serves 4–6)

Traditionally the first gooseberry pie of the season was always served on Whit Sunday—but, whenever it is, it's always something to look forward to each year.

2 lb gooseberries
6 oz sugar
6 oz plain flour
3 oz lard
1 oz margarine
A pinch of salt
A little milk

Pre-heat the oven to mark 7/425 °F

For this you'll need a 1½-pint oval pie dish—or an oblong enamelled one of the same capacity. Just top and tail the gooseberries, then pile them into the pie dish and sprinkle the sugar in amongst them. Now make up the pastry: roll it out, cut a rim to fit the dish and dampen it. Press it in place, then dampen the rim and fit the lid on over it, knocking and fluting the edges. Make a steam hole (about the size of a 10p piece) in the centre, brush the surface of the pastry with milk and sprinkle just a trace more sugar over. Bake the pie in the oven for 10 minutes, then lower the heat to mark 5/375 °F and bake for a further 30 minutes.

Spiced Bread and Apple Pudding

(Serves 4)

This is another useful way of using up stale bread, especially if you have a few windfall apples around.

About 5 or 6 medium slices wholemeal bread from a small loaf, buttered and with the crusts left on
2 medium cooking apples
2 oz demerara sugar
1 teaspoon mixed spice
1 oz currants
2 eggs
½ pint milk
Freshly grated nutmeg
A little butter

Pre-heat the oven to mark 4/350 °F

First cut the slices of bread and butter in two, and arrange half of these (buttered side down) around the base of a 1½-pint baking dish. Sprinkle in half the currants, then peel and slice the apples (fairly thinly) and pile them in on top of the bread, sprinkling in the mixed spice and about two-thirds of the sugar. Now top with the rest of the pieces of bread (buttered side uppermost this time) and sprinkle in the rest of the currants and lots of freshly grated nutmeg and the rest of the sugar. Next whisk the eggs and beat them into the ½ pint of milk; pour this over everything, add a few flecks of butter, place the dish on the highest shelf of the oven and bake the pudding for about 30–40 minutes. The top will be golden and crusty and the underneath light and puffy; and, in my opinion, it doesn't need any cream.

Making Yoghurt at Home

Without going into all the bacteriological background of yoghurt cultures and so on, let me say just one thing: if you—and more important your family as well—eat yoghurt on a fairly regular basis, then it really is far cheaper to make it yourself (and far nicer to eat when it's homemade).

Having said that, however, I also think that making yoghurt without the help of a commercially designed yoghurt-maker is rather a hit-and-miss affair—inasmuch as you do need the right sort of 'warm place' and the correct type of ventilation etc. Therefore, I recommend you invest in a modest little yoghurt-making kit. The cheapest on the market happens to be excellent (I wouldn't be without mine): this is called the Deva Bridge Yoghurt Kit and is available by post only from Deva Bridge House, Dept. W.H. PO Box 5, Stowmarket, Suffolk (at the time of writing it is £4·75 plus 48p postage and packing, but write and check the current price before ordering one). The kit consists of an insulated jar, a special thermometer and a milk saver for simmering the milk—no electricity is needed and it makes delicious yoghurt.

Then, if you keep making yoghurt regularly, you'll never be short of a pudding course. I like thick yoghurt made with milk that has been reduced from 1 pint to about ¾ pint (by simmering for 25 minutes), chilled and then served with a dollop of runny honey—the way it's eaten in Greece. Similarly, it's delicious made into fruit yoghurts, with crushed soft fruits like strawberries, raspberries, red or blackcurrants or blackberries.

In the winter I make fruit yoghurt with chopped dried prunes or apricots, soaked then cooked, or I simply serve it with chopped apples, pears or oranges, or with a fruit salad. The variations are endless—no doubt you'll think of plenty of your own. But the marvellous thing about all of them is that they're so much better for us than all the starchy, sugary foods —and happily much cheaper!

Wholemeal Bread Pudding (Serves 4)

6 oz stale wholemeal bread, grated into crumbs (in a liquidiser)
8 fl. oz milk
2 oz currants
1 oz raisins
1½ oz candied peel, finely chopped
1½ oz shredded suet
1½ oz soft brown sugar
Grated rind of ½ lemon
Grated rind of ½ orange
1 level teaspoon mixed spice
½ level teaspoon ground cinnamon
¼ whole nutmeg, grated
1 large egg, beaten
A little butter

Put the breadcrumbs into a mixing bowl, pour the milk over
them and mix thoroughly, then leave them to soak for about
30 minutes. Then stir in all the other ingredients, including
the beaten egg, and mix very thoroughly. You should have a
nice dropping consistency—if not, add a spot more milk.
Finally spread the mixture evenly into a well-buttered 1- or
1½-pint baking dish and bake it at mark 4/350°F for about an
hour.

Spotted Dick

(Serves 4)

A very comforting pudding this, especially with some warmed golden syrup poured over before serving.

8 oz self-raising flour
4 oz butter
6 oz currants
2 oz caster sugar
2 standard eggs
A little milk
A pinch salt
Some extra butter

First of all sift the flour and salt into a basin, and rub in the butter until the mixture looks nice and crumbly. Now stir in the sugar and the currants. Beat the eggs well, then add them a little at a time, stirring after each addition until the mixture is smooth. Add a little milk so that the mixture has a consistency where it will drop easily off the spoon. Pile the mixture into a 2-pint pudding basin (generously buttered) and cover with a sheet of greaseproof paper and a pleated sheet of foil. Tie securely with string, then steam in a steamer over simmering water for $2\frac{1}{2}$ hours.

Prune and Apricot Jelly

(Serves 4)

Because homemade jelly is such a rarity I think this one is special enough to serve at a dinner party.

4 oz dried prunes
4 oz dried apricots
1 strip of orange peel
Juice of 1 orange
1 small piece cinnamon stick
2 oz sugar
1 level tablespoon powdered gelatine

Start this off the night before by putting the dried prunes and apricots to soak in a pint of cold water. Then, when you're ready to make the jelly, pour the fruit (and the water they were soaked in) into a saucepan, adding the sugar, cinnamon and orange peel, and simmer gently for 20 minutes. Next fit a sieve over a bowl, pour the fruits into it and let them drain thoroughly. Then pour the liquid into a measuring jug, and add the orange juice and enough water to make it up to a pint. At this stage taste to check there's enough sugar. Now put 3 tablespoons of the liquid into a small bowl, sprinkle in the gelatine and, when it has absorbed all the liquid, fit the bowl over a saucepan of barely simmering water. Stir now and then, and when the gelatine has dissolved and become quite transparent, strain it back into the rest of the mixture, mixing it in thoroughly. Now take the stones out of the prunes, and chop all the flesh of the fruits up roughly and arrange it in the base of a 2-pint mould. Pour the gelatine mixture over the fruit, and leave in a cool place to set.

Blackberry Cheese Cake (Serves 10)

This cheese cake will serve 10 people, or last a family a whole weekend, and using curd cheese instead of cream cheese makes it much more economical.

1 lb curd cheese (Sainsburys)
4 standard eggs
1 teaspoon vanilla essence
5 oz caster sugar
2 teaspoons lemon juice

For the base and topping:
8 gingernut biscuits
8 digestive biscuits
3 oz butter (melted)
1 level teaspoon ground cinnamon
¾ lb blackberries
3 tablespoons caster sugar
2 teaspoons arrowroot mixed with 1 tablespoon water
1 extra digestive biscuit

Pre-heat the oven to mark 3/325 °F

You will need an 8½-inch cake tin with a loose base for this. Put the first lot of ingredients into a mixing bowl and whizz with an electric mixer until absolutely smooth. Then crush the biscuits—a rolling pin and a flat surface will do it in seconds —scoop them into a bowl, and then mix with the cinnamon and the butter. Next press the biscuit mixture all over the base of the tin, bringing it up about ¼ inch at the edges. Pour the cheese mixture in now and bake for about 30–40 minutes, or until firm and set in the centre; then turn the oven out and leave the cheese cake there till cool. The blackberries should be washed and simmered with the caster sugar (but no water) for a very few minutes, then drained in a sieve over a bowl. Add the arrowroot-and-water mixture to the juice, bring to the boil and boil until thickened. Mix the thickened juice with the fruit and top the cake with the mixture when cool. Press some more biscuit crumbs all round the edges. Serve only when thoroughly chilled.

Note: You can, of course, use other toppings. Blackcurrants are particularly nice, or fresh raspberries or strawberries—in season.

Spiced Apple Shortcake   (Serves 6)

1½ lb Bramley cooking apples
1 oz soft brown sugar
¼ teaspoon ground cloves
1 teaspoon cinnamon
3 oz sultanas
2 tablespoons water
¼ whole nutmeg, grated

For the topping:
8 oz wholewheat flour (Allinson's)
5 oz soft brown sugar
3 oz butter
1 teaspoon baking powder

Pre-heat the oven to mark 4/350 °F

First quarter, core and peel the apples, then slice them thinly into a saucepan and mix them with the sugar, spices and sultanas; sprinkle with the water and cook gently until the apples are soft and fluffy. While that's happening, prepare the topping by mixing the flour and baking powder in a bowl. Now rub the fat into the flour until the mixture becomes crumbly. Then stir in the sugar, making sure that all the lumps are broken down. Next arrange the apple mixture in a 4-pint pie (or baking) dish. Sprinkle the crumbled mixture lightly over this and bake in the oven for 30 minutes. Serve either warm or cold.

Traditional Lemon Pancakes   (for 4)

4 oz plain flour
A pinch of salt
2 eggs
7 fl. oz milk and 3 fl. oz water (mixed together)
2 tablespoons melted butter
Some lard
4 large lemons
Some caster sugar
A 7- or 8-inch heavy frying pan.

Begin by sifting the flour and salt into a bowl, and making a well in the centre. Break the eggs into this well, then whisk the eggs incorporating a little of the flour as you do so. Then when the mixture starts to get too thick, begin adding the milk-and-water mixture a little at a time—still whisking—until it's all in and you have a smooth batter with the consistency of thin cream.

Then when you are ready to cook the pancakes, add the 2 tablespoons of melted butter and have ready a couple of plates warming in the oven (if you pop the lemons in as well, they'll squeeze more easily). Now melt a little lard in the frying pan, swirling it around to coat the whole pan and the sides and pouring out any excess fat (into a saucer). When the pan is smoking hot, pour in 2 tablespoons of batter and turn the heat down to medium. Tip the pan from side to side to make sure the batter covers the whole base and when the pancake is brown on the underneath, flip it over with a palette knife and brown the other side. Then keep it warm between your two hot plates while you're making the remainder. Serve with lemon squeezed over and some sugar sprinkled on, and roll up.

Spiced Apricot Compote (Serves 3)

Unless you're lucky enough to get your apricots picked warm from the tree, I think gentle cooking gives them much more flavour.

1 lb fresh apricots (approximately 9)—slightly under-ripe is better
1 small piece cinnamon stick
1 vanilla pod
½ pint hot water
2 tablespoons dark soft brown sugar
2 teaspoons arrowroot mixed with 1 tablespoon water

Pre-heat the oven to mark 3/325°F

First place the apricots, sugar, water and spices in a thick cooking pot (earthenware is ideal), cover them tightly, place in the oven and let them cook for about ¾–1 hour depending on their ripeness—they need to be cooked until tender but not disintegrating. When they're cooked, remove the apricots to a serving dish using a draining spoon. Then pour the juices into a small saucepan and extract the spices. Now bring the juices up to simmering point, mix the arrowroot with 1 tablespoon of cold water till smooth, add it to the juices, bring back to simmering point and continue to simmer until the mixture has thickened to a syrupy consistency. Then pour the sauce over the apricots and serve either warm or chilled.

Weighing

Liquids

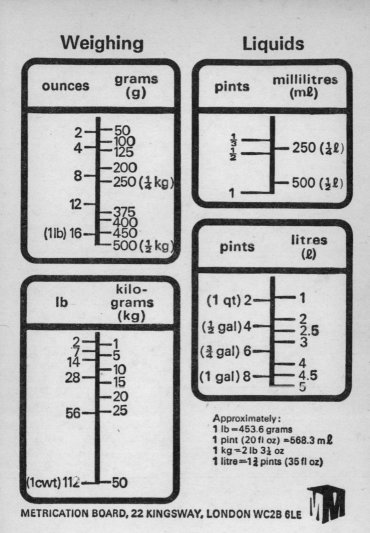

Weighing

ounces	grams (g)
2	50
	100
4	125
	200
8	250 (¼ kg)
12	
	375
	400
(1 lb) 16	450
	500 (½ kg)

lb	kilo-grams (kg)
2	1
7	5
14	10
28	15
	20
56	25
(1 cwt) 112	50

Liquids

pints	millilitres (mℓ)
¼	
½	250 (¼ ℓ)
1	500 (½ ℓ)

pints	litres (ℓ)
(1 qt) 2	1
(½ gal) 4	2
	2.5
	3
(¾ gal) 6	4
(1 gal) 8	4.5
	5

Approximately :
1 lb = 453.6 grams
1 pint (20 fl oz) = 568.3 mℓ
1 kg = 2 lb 3¼ oz
1 litre = 1¾ pints (35 fl oz)

METRICATION BOARD, 22 KINGSWAY, LONDON WC2B 6LE

INDEX

NOTES

NOTES

NOTES

NOTES

NOTES

NOTES

NOTES

NOTES

NOTES